Mary Royer

Picture-Story LIFE OF CHRIST

Adapted from *Bible Story Book*

By Elsie E. Egermeier

THE WARNER PRESS
Anderson, Indiana

Library of Congress Catalog Card No. 58-8409

Revised Edition—1958

Lithographed in United States of America

Preface

Towering above all the characters whom the world calls great stands one Person—Jesus Christ. Everybody should know about him.

Adults find the record of his marvelous life in the Book of books. There, in language familiar to them, they read all about him, and they conclude that he was the greatest, the kindest, and the most helpful Person this world has ever known.

Children, too, should be given the opportunity to read about him. And so, because picture-language is more familiar to children, and story-language is more easily understood by them, we present here in pictures and stories a record of the Life of Christ.

Elsie E. Egermeier

THE GOOD SHEPHERD

JESUS ON THE MOUNTAIN

Contents

List of Pictures

Picture-Story Life of Christ

STORY 1

A Wonderful Baby's Birth

Luke 2:1-39

Out on the streets of Nazareth the people were standing in groups, talking excitedly. News had just reached their city that the great emperor of Rome had commanded all of them to go to the town or city from which their families had come and have their names written on lists. The emperor wished to have a list of the names of all the people in his great kingdom, or empire. And no one dared to disobey his command.

Soon travelers were seen going in every direction, for the emperor's command had been read in every city in the land. Out from Nazareth a company of people started toward the south, and in that company were Joseph and Mary, for they were both of the family of David, and they were going to Bethlehem, the city of David, to have their names written upon the list there.

The road to the south led through the country of Samaria, then over the hills of Judea into Jerusalem.

From Jerusalem Joseph and Mary went farther south, till they came to Bethlehem. Some of their company had left them in other cities along the way, while others had joined them. And when they reached Bethlehem they found that it was swarming with people who belonged, as they did, to the city where David was born. From every part of the land these people had come, and they had filled the lodging rooms till no more place could be found for the new arrivals.

The long journey from Nazareth had been very tiresome, and Mary longed for a place to rest. But Joseph could find no place except in the stable of the inn. And one night while they stayed here the baby Jesus was born. Mary wrapped him in soft cloths called swaddling clothes, and laid him in a manger where the cattle fed, because she could find no better place.

Shepherds were watching their flocks that night in a field near Bethlehem. Perhaps David, the shepherd king, had tended sheep in that same field many years before. These shepherds knew about David, and about God's promise to David that one of his descendants would be the Savior of men. And they may have been talking about God's promise when the angel of the Lord suddenly came near and a glorious light broke upon them through the darkness. Trembling with fear, they looked upon the angel and wondered why he had come to them. Then he spoke, and said: "Fear not, for I bring you good tidings of great joy, which shall be to all people. For unto you is born this day in the city of David a Savior, which is Christ the Lord. And you will find the baby wrapped in swaddling clothes and lying in a manger."

What a wonderful message! The shepherds listened eagerly to the angel's words, and when he finished speaking they saw a multitude of angels join him and begin to sing. Such music this world had never heard, for the angels were singing one of heaven's glad songs, giving glory to God in the highest. And they also sang, "Peace on earth, good will toward men."

When the song had ended, the angels went back into heaven and the glorious light faded again into the darkness of the still night. But the shepherds never forgot the sweetness of that song nor the joy it brought to their hearts. They did not wait until daylight to hasten to Bethlehem in search of the wonderful child. Just as soon as the angels disappeared they said to each other, "Let us now go to Bethlehem and see this thing which the Lord has made known to us." So they left their flocks and hurried to Bethlehem. There they found Mary and Joseph in the stable, with the infant Savior lying in the manger, as the angel had said.

The shepherds told Mary and Joseph about their angel visitors and about the wonderful song that the angels sang. And no doubt they knelt before the manger and worshiped the little babe who lay quietly sleeping in the hay. Then they ran into the streets of Bethlehem and told every one whom they met about the angels' visit and about the wonderful child who had been born that night in a stable. And the people wondered about the strange things that the shepherds told.

When the baby was eight days old Joseph and Mary gave him a name, and they called him by the name the angel had chosen. That name, Jesus, means "salvation," and it told to men the work that God had sent this child to do.

There was a law among the Jews that an offering should be made to the Lord for the first boy child born into each family. Among the rich people this offering should be a lamb, but among the poor people the offering of only two young pigeons would please God just as well. When Jesus was forty days old Joseph and Mary took him to the Temple at Jerusalem to give their offering to the Lord. They brought two pigeons, for they were poor and could not bring a lamb.

An old man named Simeon was in the Temple when Joseph and Mary came to bring their offering. This old man had served God for many years, and he wanted to see the Savior whom God had promised to send into the world. God knew about this longing in Simeon's heart, and one day he spoke to Simeon and said, "You shall not die until you have seen the Savior."

When Mary brought the baby Jesus to the Temple, God's Spirit caused Simeon to know this child was the promised Savior. He came eagerly to meet Mary and took her baby in his arms. Then he said, "Now may God

MARY HOLDING THE BABY JESUS

THE JOURNEY TO JERUSALEM

let me depart in peace, for I have seen with my eyes the salvation which he has sent."

Another faithful servant of the Lord was in the Temple that day. She was an old lady named Anna, who spoke words of prophecy to the people. When she saw Jesus she gave thanks to God. And to the people who stood in the courts of the Temple she spoke about this child of promise which had been sent from God to man.

Mary never forgot the words of these dear old people concerning her wonderful child. She remembered, too, the story that the shepherds had told about the angels' visit to them and about their words and song. In the days that followed Mary always thought about these strange things and wondered how her son Jesus would finally become the King and Savior of the world.

Questions and Answers

1. Why did Joseph and Mary journey to Bethlehem? (As descendants of David, they were required to register for taxation in that city.)
2. Where did they find lodging when they came into Bethlehem? (In the stable of the inn.)
3. Why did the angels watch over Bethlehem one night while Mary and Joseph were there? (Because Jesus, the Savior, was born on that night.)
4. Who heard the glorious song the angels sang? (Shepherds in a field.)
5. Where did the shepherds go after they had heard the angel? (To Bethlehem.)

STORY 2

The Wise Men Follow a Star

Matthew 2

In the country far to the east of Judea there lived some wise men who studied the stars. One night they discovered a new star in the sky, one that they had never seen before. And God caused them to know by this star that Christ, the promised King of the Jews, had been born.

These wise men feared God, and they wished to see the child whom he had sent to be the Savior of the world. They supposed that the Jews must be very happy because God had at last sent to them the King he had promised.

Because these wise men were rich, they planned at once to make the long journey to Judea and bring precious gifts to the newborn King. Then they would worship him as their Savior.

For many days they traveled across the sandy desert, and at last they came to the fertile country where the Jews lived. They hurried on to the city of Jerusalem, for they expected to find the wonderful child living in the most beautiful place in all the land. And surely the famous city would be the most beautiful place.

THE WISE MEN FOLLOW THE STAR

Herod, the man whom the emperor of Rome had made king over the land of Judea, was living in Jerusalem at that time. He was surprised when these strangers, riding on camels, came into his city and asked, "Where is the child that is born King of the Jews? We have seen his star in the far east country, and have come to worship him." Herod had heard nothing about this newborn King, and he was troubled. "What can this mean?" he wondered. And even the rich people in Jerusalem were puzzled too. They had heard nothing about Jesus.

The wise men were disappointed when they found that the rulers of Jerusalem knew nothing about the birth of the Savior. Perhaps they feared that they might have been mistaken, after all. But they waited anxiously while Herod called the chief priests and the scribes and asked them where the Savior should be born.

Now the chief priests and scribes were the men who read the books that the prophets had written long ago, and they understood that Christ should be born in Bethlehem. They told this to the excited Herod.

Herod was worried. He thought this newborn King would take away his throne, and he wished to be king himself. But he did not let the wise men know about his fears. He called them and asked very politely when they had first seen this unusual star in the east, and they told him. Then he urged them to hurry on to Bethlehem and search diligently to find the child. "When you have found him," said Herod, "bring me word at once, that I, too, may go and worship him." And with these words he dismissed them from his presence.

The wise men mounted their camels again and took the south road, leading to Bethlehem. All day they had waited impatiently in Jerusalem, and now the shadows of night were falling over the land. But it would not be a very long ride to the birthplace of the newborn King, and, urged on by Herod's words, they hastened to find Jesus. When they were once outside the city gates they saw the star, the same beautiful star that had shown so brightly in the east country, moving slowly before them, as if leading them on to the right place. Now they were sure that they had not been mistaken; and they rejoiced greatly, for they believed that God was in this manner trying to help them to find Jesus.

When they reached Bethlehem the star stood still over the place where Mary and Joseph were living. And the wise men knew they had followed the right guide, for here they found the wonderful child of whom the prophets had written. They knelt in humble worship before him, and then gave to him the rich treasures that they had brought from their homeland.

God spoke to the wise men in a dream one night while they were in Bethlehem, and warned them not to tell Herod that they had found Jesus. So they returned to their own country by another road, and Herod never saw them again. Not long afterwards an angel of the Lord spoke to Joseph in a dream, and said, "Arise, and take the young child and his mother, and flee into Egypt, and stay there until I bring word to you to return again; for Herod will seek for Jesus and try to destroy him."

Joseph rose up at once, and while it was yet dark he took Mary and the baby Jesus and hurried out of Bethlehem. For many days they traveled to the southwest, until they came to the land of Egypt. There they lived until an angel came to tell them that the wicked Herod was dead.

But Herod did not die for some time after the visit of the wise men. He waited long for them to return, bringing him word from Bethlehem as he had commanded them to do. But when many days passed and they did not come, he began to suspect that they had gone home without telling him of their wonderful discovery in Bethlehem. He believed they had guessed the reason why he had been so eager to see Jesus, and now he was angry because he had missed this opportunity to find the newborn King of the Jews.

Determined to destroy this King of the prophecies, Herod commanded his soldiers to go to Bethlehem and kill every baby there from two years old and younger. He sent them not only to Bethlehem but also to the country places round about. And when this cruel deed was done he believed that he had surely gotten rid of this child whom the wise men sought to worship.

But all the while Jesus was living in safety among the people of Egypt, and fast growing out of his babyhood years. Then the wicked Herod died, and an angel came again to speak to Joseph, telling him to return with his wife and her child to their own land.

Joseph was glad to receive this message from the angel, for he loved to live among his own people. And he started back to Bethlehem. But when he came into Judea he heard that Herod's son was now the ruler of the Jews in Judea, and he feared that this new king might be like his father. Because of this fear Joseph journeyed on to Nazareth, in the country of Galilee, where he and Mary had lived before Jesus was born. And there he made a home for his wife and her wonderful child.

Questions and Answers

1. What wonderful meaning did the new star have to the wise men in the east? (They believed it announced the birth of the Messiah.)

2. Why did these wise men decide to journey to Judea? (They wanted to worship the newborn King of the Jews.)

3. From whom, in Jerusalem, did the wise men inquire about the newborn King of the Jews? (Herod, who was the king at that time.)

4. What request did King Herod make of the wise men when he sent them away to Bethlehem? ("Bring me word at once when you have found the child.")

5. How did God help the wise men to find the baby Jesus? (The star led them to the place where Joseph and Mary were living.)

THE BOY JESUS IN THE CARPENTER SHOP

STORY 3

When Jesus Was a Boy

Luke 2:40-52

Nazareth, the boyhood home of Jesus, was nearly seventy miles from Jerusalem. The Jews who lived in this city could not go every week to worship God at the Temple, so they built a house of worship, called a synagogue, in their home town. Here they attended religious services, and listened to the reading of the books written by Moses and by the prophets.

As a little boy, Jesus lived in the humble home of Joseph, the carpenter, and played among the shavings that fell from Joseph's bench. He also liked to run about and play in the warm sunshine, as little children do today. But when he grew old enough to go to school his parents sent him to the synagogue, where other Jewish boys were taught to read and to write.

We are sure that Jesus studied his lessons well and that he gave careful attention to the books he read each day. These books were copies of the Psalms and of the writings of Moses, the lawgiver, and the prophets. Like other Jewish boys, he learned to repeat many of these Scriptures from memory, for he never had a Bible of his own, such as many children have today.

One spring morning after Jesus was twelve years old a company of Jews started from Nazareth to attend the Feast of the Passover, at Jerusalem. Every year since their return from Egypt, Joseph and Mary had attended this Feast, and now, as usual, they were in this company. But this time they were taking with them for the first time the boy Jesus.

Other children, too, were going. They would enjoy the long trip of nearly seventy miles much more than would their parents and grown-up friends.

As the company moved slowly along the road, other Jews from cities and villages near by joined them. And when they came to Jerusalem they met people from every part of the land. What an exciting time this must have been for the children! How wide their eyes must have opened when they saw the beautiful Temple on Mount Moriah, with its wide porches and immense pillars of stone! And perhaps they stayed close by their parents during the first days of the Feast, lest they should get lost in the throng of people who daily crowded the Temple courts.

Jesus enjoyed this Feast as much as did his parents and grown-up friends. Although just a child, he was beginning to realize that God was his Father and that he must work for God. So he listened to the readings of the law and to the words of the chief priests and scribes, who taught the Jews every day. But we are sure that he acted very much like a healthy twelve-year-old boy, for his mother did not notice how deeply interested he had been in the services at the Temple.

After the Feast had ended the company started on its homeward journey. Mary did not see her young son; but since she supposed that he was among their kinsfolk and friends, she did not feel uneasy. However, when at evening he did not come, she and Joseph began to search for him. All through the company they went, asking about Jesus; but no one had seen him that day. Then they turned with anxious faces back toward Jerusalem, and for three days they searched for their missing child.

On the third day they found him. He was not playing with other boys in the streets, nor learning to swim in the Pool of Siloam, but sitting in the Temple among the wise teachers, listening to them and asking them questions which they could hardly answer.

Mary was surprised when she found Jesus in the Temple among the wise men. She had looked every other place for him. She knew he was just a boy, and she was surprised to find him so deeply interested in the teachings of God. She came to him and said, "Son, why did you stay here when we were starting home? Your father and I have been anxiously seeking for you everywhere."

Jesus answered, "Why did you seek for me? Did you not know that I must be about my Father's business?"

He meant, "Why did you not know where to find me at once? For I must be learning about my heavenly

Father's work." But Mary did not understand, though she wondered much about the meaning of his words.

The teachers in the Temple had been much surprised to hear the wisdom of the boy Jesus. They had gathered round him to ask questions that only wise persons could answer. And Jesus answered them, every one.

But when Mary and Joseph came to the Temple, Jesus left the teachers there and returned with his parents to Nazareth. He was an obedient child, and as the years passed by he grew into a noble young man. He learned how to explain the Scriptures, and he helped Joseph at his work until he, too, became a carpenter. And by his kind, thoughtful ways he won many friends. In this humble home in Nazareth, Jesus lived until he was about thirty years old.

Questions and Answers

1. Why did Joseph and Mary take Jesus on this journey to the Temple? (He was now twelve years old.)

2. How did Jesus happen to be left behind when Joseph and Mary started home? (They thought he was somewhere in their company.)

3. For how many days did they search before they found Jesus? (Three.)

4. What was Jesus doing when they found him? (He was asking questions of the wise teachers in the Temple.)

5. Why did he return with Joseph and Mary to their home in Nazareth? (Because he was an obedient boy.)

JOHN THE BAPTIST

STORY 4

The Strange Preacher

Matthew 3; Mark 1:2-11; Luke 3:1-23; John 1:15-34

While Jesus was growing to manhood in the city of Nazareth, in Galilee, John, the son of a priest named Zacharias, was growing to manhood in the desert country of Judea. John spent much of his time alone in this desert country, listening to God's voice. And when he became a man he left his lonely home in the desert and began to tell God's words to the people.

John did not go to the cities to preach God's message, but stayed in the wilderness of Judea near the Jordan River. And the people came from every part of the land to hear him speak. There had been no prophet among the Jews since the days of Malachi, more than four hundred years before, and now everybody was eager to hear this strange preacher in the wilderness tell the words that God had spoken to him. They believed he was a prophet sent from God, and they came in great numbers to hear his words.

And John's words were indeed wonderful. He told the people that they should turn away from their sins and begin to do right, for God's kingdom was near at hand. He said that the King for whom they had been looking would soon come among them. And those who confessed their sins he baptized in the river. For this reason they called him "John the Baptist."

All classes of people came to John to be baptized by him. Among them were even the religious rulers of the Jews—the Pharisees and the Sadducees. These men were very careful to appear righteous before others. But God, who looked into their hearts, saw that they were proud and sinful. God saw that they despised the poor unfortunate people who lived among them and that they believed themselves to be more righteous than other men. When they came to be baptized by John, God caused him to know that these Pharisees and Sadducees were only making believe that they were good. So John said to them, "Who has warned you evil men to flee from God's wrath? You cannot be prepared to enter God's kingdom until you first turn away from your sins."

John taught the people who came to him that they should be unselfish and be kind to the poor. He told those who were rich to share their food and their clothing with the needy. He told those who were soldiers to harm no one and to be contented with their wages. He tried in this way to teach them that God's kingdom would be a kingdom of love and peace and "good will toward men," just as the angels sang to the shepherds on the night of Jesus' birth.

News of the strange preacher in the wilderness spread even to the farthest corners of the land, and everywhere the people were talking about his message. They were wondering whether John was the prophet Elijah come back to earth again, for John did not dress like other men. He wore a rough garment woven of camel's hair, tied about his waist with a skin girdle. And he ate the simple food that he found in the wilderness, dried locusts and wild honey. And he was bold, as Elijah had been, and unafraid to speak the truth even to the wicked King Herod.

When John heard about the wonderings of the people, he said, "I am the voice of one crying in the wilderness, warning you to prepare for the coming King. After me there is coming One greater than I—so much greater that I am not worthy to unfasten his shoes. And though I baptize you with water, he shall baptize you with the Holy Spirit, sent down from heaven."

After these things happened, one day Jesus came from Nazareth to the Jordan River, where John was preaching and baptizing the people. And Jesus asked to be baptized also. John did not believe that Jesus needed to be baptized, and he said, "You are so much greater than I that I should be baptized by you. Why do you come to me?"

Jesus answered, "It is necessary that I should be baptized by you, because this is God's plan."

So John took Jesus into the river and baptized him.

When these two were coming up out of the water, suddenly the heavens opened above them and the Spirit of God, in the form of a beautiful dove, came down and sat upon Jesus' head. Then a voice from heaven said, "This is my beloved Son, in whom I am well pleased." John knew by this sign who Jesus was; for God had told him that some day he would see the heavens open and the Spirit of God descend upon the coming King.

After this time John continued to preach, and sometimes Herod heard him. Although Herod was troubled because John told him about his sins, his wife was much displeased with this fearless preacher of the wilderness. She wanted her husband, Herod, to kill him. And to please her, Herod shut John up in prison.

Questions and Answers

1. Why was the wilderness preacher called John the Baptist? (Because he baptized people in the Jordan River.)

2. Of what great prophet did John remind the people? (The bold prophet Elijah.)

3. Why did Jesus ask John to baptize him? (He knew God wanted him to receive John's baptism.)

4. By what sign did John know that Jesus was God's promised Savior? (The Spirit of God in the form of a dove alighted on Jesus' head.)

STORY 5

Jesus Is Tempted

Matt. 4:1-11; Mark 1:12, 13; Luke 4:1-14

After the baptism in the Jordan River, when God's voice spoke from heaven, and said, "This is my beloved Son," Jesus was led by the Spirit of God into the lonely wilderness. There he lived by himself for forty days, among the wild beasts. But God did not allow any harm to come to him.

Satan, the tempter, found Jesus all alone in the wilderness. And he tried first in one way and then in another to get Jesus to listen to his cunning plans and open his heart to let sin enter. But Jesus would not listen.

When the forty days were ended, Jesus grew very faint and hungry, for he had eaten nothing since he came into this lonely place. Then Satan said, "If you really are the Son of God, command that these stones become loaves of bread." He thought Jesus would surely yield to this temptation and try to prove that he was God's Son. But Jesus answered, "Man shall not live by bread only, but by every word of God."

Although he was hungry and faint, Jesus would not use his great power to please himself. He was willing to trust his heavenly Father to care for him in that desert

JESUS BEING TEMPTED

place and to supply his needs. When Satan saw that he could not cause Jesus to yield to this temptation, he tried another.

He said, "If you expect people to believe that you are really God's Son, you must show some great sign. Now cast yourself down to the ground from the topmost part of the Temple in Jerusalem. God will protect you and keep your bones from being broken. In the Scripture he has promised that angels will bear you up and not allow any harm to befall you."

Even though Satan used Scripture to urge Jesus to do this foolish thing, yet Jesus would not obey him. For Jesus knew that the Scriptures had forbidden anyone to tempt God in such a foolish manner and expect God's angels to help him. Again Satan saw that his plan had failed.

The third time Satan brought his greatest temptation. He said to Jesus, "All the great kingdoms of the world are mine, and I can give them to anyone I choose. Now I will give them to you if only you will fall down and worship me."

But Jesus knew that Satan's words were not true. He said, "Get away from me, you evil one! for it is written in the Scriptures that the Lord God is the only Being who should be worshiped."

Then Satan left Jesus alone; for he could find no way to crowd sin into the pure heart of the Son of God. And when he went away the angels came from heaven and supplied Jesus' needs. How they must have rejoiced because the Savior had gained such a victory over the evil one!

Jesus was tempted in every way that people on the earth are tempted; still he did no wrong. By his temptations he was made to understand how people feel when Satan whispers to their hearts and urges them to sin, and he understands how to help those people when they call upon him in prayer.

Questions and Answers

1. Who found Jesus alone in the wilderness? (Satan, the tempter.)
2. How long had Jesus been without food? (Forty days.)
3. Why would not Jesus turn stones into bread? (Jesus would not use his great power to please himself.)
4. Why did Satan want Jesus to cast himself down from the top of the Temple? (To prove that he is the Son of God.)
5. What did Satan promise to give to Jesus if he would fall down and worship him? (All the kingdoms of the world.)

STORY 6

Five Men Become Acquainted with Jesus

John 1:35-51

Many people who heard John preach by the riverside believed his words, and they began to look for the coming of the King from heaven. From day to day they waited, eager to hear the glad news that the King had arrived. They believed that he would set up a kingdom in Judea. And they believed that the Jews would be the favored people in this great kingdom.

One day after Jesus had returned from the lonely wilderness, John the Baptist saw him walking along the road near the river. And John cried out, "Behold the Lamb of God, who bears the sin of the world!"

Two young men from Galilee were with John that day and heard him speak. These young men had been disciples, or learners, of John, for they were interested in the teachings of God. When they heard John's words concerning Jesus, the Lamb of God, they turned at once to follow this wonderful person. Perhaps they wondered why John had called him the "Lamb of God." And perhaps they wondered how he could bear the sin of the world. This was a mystery to them.

Jesus knew these young men were following him, so he stopped and called to them. He asked what they wanted of him, and they answered, "Master, where do you live?" Then Jesus took them with him and talked with them all that day.

We do not know what Jesus told those men, but we do know that his words proved to their minds that he was the King, or Messiah, for whom the Jews were looking. How glad they were because they had found him!

One of those young men was Andrew, who afterwards became a disciple of Jesus. Just as soon as he believed that Jesus was the promised King he remembered that his brother Simon was waiting eagerly to see this great person, too. So he hurried at once to find Simon and bring him to Jesus.

Simon and Andrew lived by the seaside in Galilee, but at this time they were numbered among the many people who daily sat listening to the words of the strange preacher in the wilderness. Never had they heard such wonderful teaching before, and they were sure that John was a prophet. But Jesus' words had convinced Andrew that he had found a new teacher who was even greater than John. So he called Simon aside from the multitude, and said, "Come with me, for we have found the Messiah!"

When Jesus saw the two brothers coming to his lodging place he looked at Simon and said, "You are Simon, the son of Jona; but you shall be called Peter."

Simon wondered how Jesus knew so much about him, but after he listened to Jesus' words he, too, believed that the long-looked-for King of the Jews had come. And with his brother Andrew he followed Jesus.

On the next day Jesus began his journey back to his home country in Galilee, and these men went with him. As they went they met a man named Philip, who lived in the same town in which Simon and Andrew lived. Jesus called Philip to follow him, too; and Philip obeyed. As he walked along the road with Jesus and the other followers, Philip listened in wonder to the wise sayings of his new-found friend. He had longed for the coming of the Messiah, and now he, too, believed that Jesus was the promised Savior and King.

Philip had a neighbor named Nathanael who had often talked with him about the glorious time when the King of the Jews would appear. And now he ran to tell Nathanael about Jesus. He knew how greatly Nathanael longed to see the coming King, and he called to him, saying, "We have found him, of whom Moses in the law, and the prophets, did write, Jesus of Nazareth."

Nathanael knew the Scriptures, and he did not believe that the King of the Jews would come from Nazareth, for the prophets had said he would be born in Bethlehem. So he said to Philip, "Can any good thing come out of Nazareth?" But Philip answered, "Come and see."

Because Philip was so eager, Nathanael rose and followed him. When they came near, Jesus saw Nathanael,

JOHN AND ANDREW FOLLOW JESUS

JESUS WITH JOHN THE BAPTIST

and he said, "Behold an Israelite indeed, in whom is no guile!"

"How do you know me?" asked the astonished Jew.

And Jesus answered, "Before Philip called you, when you were under the fig tree, I saw you."

What Nathanael had been doing under the fig tree we can only guess, but he may have been kneeling there and praying that God would hasten the coming of the promised King. When he heard Jesus' answer, he was filled with wonder and surprise that Jesus could know what he had been doing and where he had been staying before Philip called him. He believed that only God can see all things, and can reveal them to men, so he exclaimed joyfully, "Master, you are the Son of God! You are the King of Israel!"

Questions and Answers

1. What did John say of Jesus when he saw him walking by? ("Behold the Lamb of God, who bears the sin of the world.")

2. Why did two of John's disciples follow Jesus that day? (They wanted to learn more about him.)

3. Who brought Simon to Jesus? (His brother, Andrew.)

4. What new name did Jesus give to him? (Peter.)

5. Why did Philip become a follower of Jesus? (He believed that Jesus was the Messiah whom God had promised.)

6. Whom did Philip then bring to Jesus? (His friend Nathanael.)

STORY 7

Jesus at a Wedding Feast

John 2:1-11

In Cana, a little town in Galilee, lived some friends of Jesus and his mother. One day these friends invited Jesus, his mother, and his followers to attend a wedding in their home. They invited many other people also and prepared a feast for them.

Perhaps these people were poor; for they had not prepared enough wine for all the people who came. The wine was soon all gone.

Mary, the mother of Jesus, saw that the wine had all been used, and she called Jesus aside to tell him about it. She knew of his wonderful power, and she believed he could surely help in a time like this. Then she told the servants who waited at the tables to do whatever Jesus might command them.

In every Jewish home there were large vessels, called waterpots, which the people kept filled with water to use in washing their hands and their feet. In this home where the wedding feast was being held there were six large stone waterpots.

Jesus called the servants and told them to fill the waterpots with water. And remembering his mother's

JESUS COMMANDING THE WATERPOTS TO BE FILLED

instructions to them, the servants drew water and filled the vessels to the brim. Then Jesus told them to draw out from the vessels and fill their wine pitchers again. When they obeyed they saw that wine flowed from the vessels they had just filled with water.

At these Jewish feasts one man was chosen to be the governor, or ruler, of the feast. He tasted the food and the wine before it was placed on the tables to serve the people. Jesus told the servants to take this wine to the governor and have him taste it, just as he had tasted the first wine that had been served to the guests.

Now the governor did not know what Jesus had done. He did not know that the other wine had all been used and there was no more to be had. When he tasted the wine which Jesus had made from water he was surprised because it was so much better than the first wine which had been served. Calling the young man who had just been married, the governor said, "At other wedding feasts the best wine is served first, but you have kept the best until the last of the feast."

This was the first miracle Jesus performed, and it showed his willingness to help people who are in need.

Questions and Answers

1. Where did Jesus perform his first miracle? (Cana, a town in Galilee.)

2. Why were the servants careful to do just as Jesus had bidden them? (Because Mary, his mother, told them to do this.)

3. What did the governor of the feast say about the wine which Jesus had made? (That it was the best they served at the feast.)

STORY 8

The Great Teacher in Jerusalem

John 2:13—3:21

The time had come again for the yearly Passover feast in Jerusalem, and from every part of the land groups of people came flocking to attend this great religious meeting.

In one of these groups were Jesus and his friends, Andrew, Simon, Philip, and Nathanael. These men were called his disciples, or learners, for they often went with him from one place to another to learn more about his wonderful teachings.

Only the priests were allowed to enter the rooms of the Temple, and the people who went there to worship stood in the courts outside the rooms and prayed while the priests offered sacrifices upon the altars.

When Jesus came with his disciples and friends to attend the Feast of the Passover, he found much disorder in the court where the people were supposed to worship God. This beautiful court looked more like a market place than like a house of prayer, for men had brought oxen and sheep and doves in there to sell for sacrifices to those who came from distant places to worship God.

And other men, who were called money-changers, were sitting by small tables exchanging pieces of silver money, called half shekels, for the coins people brought from distant lands. Every Jew, we are told, who was twenty years old or older, gave one of these half shekels to the priests each year to buy sacrifices and to supply other needs in the Temple worship. No other coins except half shekels could be received by the priests, so the Jews who came from other lands had to exchange their coins for half shekels before they could pay their dues to the priests.

Jesus was grieved to see the disorder in the Temple court. He knew that worshipers could not enjoy praying in such a noisy place, where buying and selling and money-exchanging were going on around them. So he made a whip by tying small cords together, and then he drove out the oxen and sheep and the men who kept them. He even upset the tables of the money-changers, and he told them that his Father's house was a place of prayer and should not be used for a market place.

No doubt other people had been grieved to see the disorder in the Temple court at the time of the Passover feast. But none of them had ever dared to do what Jesus did. None of them had courage enough to try to correct this great evil.

But not all of the Jews were pleased to see Jesus drive the money lovers and the owners of the oxen and sheep and doves into the streets outside the Temple. Some of

JESUS TALKING WITH NICODEMUS

them came to Jesus and asked him for a sign to prove that he was some great man with authority to do such things. Jesus knew they would not accept him, even when they should see a sign, so he answered, "Destroy this temple, and in three days I will raise it." He spoke about himself, meaning his body, which he knew the Jews would cause to be crucified, and which he would raise up from the dead after three days.

But the Jews did not understand, and they thought he meant the Temple on Mount Moriah, which Herod, the king, had rebuilt for them. They said, "Many years were spent in building this Temple, and you say you could rebuild it in three days!" Then they shook their heads doubtfully and walked away, for they did not believe his words.

At this Feast Jesus began to teach the people and to do miracles among them. And many believed in him when they heard his words and saw the great works which no other man could do.

One of those who believed in Jesus was a ruler among the Jews, a Pharisee. His name was Nicodemus, and he was a very rich man. There were many Pharisees among the Jewish rulers, and these men were proud and unwilling to accept either John the Baptist or Jesus as being teachers sent from God. They themselves wished to be the religious leaders of the Jews, and they despised humble men like John and Jesus. But Nicodemus was not like his proud friends. He heard Jesus teach the

JESUS GOING INTO THE SYNAGOGUE TO WORSHIP

JESUS CALLING PETER AND ANDREW

people who had come to worship at the Feast, and he believed that surely Jesus was some great man.

While the other Pharisees were finding fault with Jesus, Nicodemus longed to hear more of his teachings. One night he came to the place where Jesus stayed while he was in Jerusalem, and asked to have a talk with this man from Galilee.

Jesus received Nicodemus gladly, and talked to him about the kingdom of God. He told this ruler that no man could enter God's kingdom unless he should be born again. Nicodemus wondered how this could be possible, so Jesus explained to him the secret of the new birth, which we call a change of heart. Never before had this wise ruler of the Jews heard such strange words, and he listened wonderingly while Jesus told about the great love of God. "This love," said Jesus, "caused God to give his only Son, that whoever believes in him may not die because of sin, but have life forevermore."

Then Jesus reminded Nicodemus of the story of Moses in the wilderness when the people had sinned and God had sent fiery snakes into their camp. Nicodemus remembered the story, and Jesus said, "Just as those people who were about to die from the snake bites found relief from their pain by looking at the brass snake that Moses put upon a pole in their camp, so the people who have sin in their hearts may find relief from sin by looking at the Son of Man, who shall be raised up among them." Nicodemus did not understand that Jesus was speaking about the cruel way in which he should sometime be put to death to save the people from their sins. But Nicodemus did believe more strongly than ever that Jesus was a great teacher who had come down from heaven to dwell among men.

Faith in Jesus as the Redeemer of the world gives everlasting life.

Questions and Answers

1. What did Jesus do when he saw the disorder in the temple court? (He drove out the oxen and the sheep and the men who kept them.)

2. For what did Jesus say that his Father's house should be used? (A place of prayer.)

3. What Pharisee wanted to become acquainted with Jesus? (Nicodemus.)

4. What did Nicodemus think of Jesus after he had visited with him? (He believed more strongly than ever that Jesus had come from God.)

STORY 9

The Tired Stranger Rests by a Well

John 4:1-43

Between Judea and Galilee was a little country called Samaria. This country used to belong to the kingdom of Israel. But when the Israelites were carried away as captives by the king of Assyria, strangers from other lands came into that country and made their homes.

These strangers learned about the God of the Israelites, but they never worshiped God at the Temple in Jerusalem. Instead, they built a temple in their country and worshiped there. They became bitter enemies of the Jews, and at the time of Jesus they still were despised by the Jews. In going to or returning from Jerusalem, the Jews of Galilee usually would not take the shorter road, through Samaria, but would travel the long road, which led first to and across the Jordan River, then along the border of Samaria.

Although Jesus was a Jew, he did not share the bitter feeling of the Jews toward the people of Samaria, who were called Samaritans. He knew they were just as precious in the eyes of God as were any other people, and he longed to teach them about the kingdom of heaven. He did not mind walking through their country on his journey back to his home in Nazareth.

Because Jesus wished to take the road through Samaria, his disciples were willing to go that way too, in order to be with him. So they journeyed together and came to a little city called Sychar.

Near the city was a wayside well, which had been dug hundreds of years before, probably by Jacob, the grandson of Abraham. And in honor of him it was still called Jacob's well. When they reached this well, Jesus was tired and sat down by it to rest from his long walk. His disciples went on to the city to buy food, leaving him there alone.

Presently a woman from Sychar came down to the well to draw some water. She glanced at the stranger sitting there and saw that he was a Jew. Knowing that Jews paid no attention to Samaritans, she passed by and hurried to lower her water jug with the long rope that she had brought. When the jug was filled she drew it up and was ready to start back to the city, when Jesus asked for a drink.

Surprised at his request, the woman answered, "How is it that you, being a Jew, will ask a drink of me, a woman of Samaria? for the Jews have no dealings with the Samaritans."

Jesus replied, "If you knew who it is who asks a drink from your jug of sparkling water, you would ask of him and he would give you living water to drink."

These words aroused the interest of the woman at once. "Who can this stranger be?" she wondered. She knew he was not like other Jews, for they would rather suffer from thirst than ask a favor of a Samaritan. "Sir," she said, "this well is deep and you have no rope to draw out the water. How then could you give me living water to drink? Are you greater than Jacob, who gave us this well, and drank of it himself, and his cattle?"

"Whoever drinks of this water in Jacob's well becomes thirsty and returns again and again for more," answered Jesus, "but the living water which I give does not come from such a well. It bubbles up like a continual spring within one, and that one never grows thirsty again."

Now the woman was an eager listener. She did not know that the living water of which Jesus spoke was his free gift of salvation to all people, and she said, "Sir, I want that kind of water so that I shall not need to return and refill my water jug in this tiresome way."

Jesus saw that she was interested, so he began to talk to her about her sins. He knew she was a very sinful woman, and he told her about some wrong things that she had done. She wondered how he, a stranger, could know these things. He seemed to see her thoughts and to read them all. "You are a prophet," she exclaimed with surprise.

Although this woman was a sinner, she wondered often whether God was more pleased with the religion of the Jews than with the religion of her own people, the

Samaritans. Now she asked Jesus whether people should worship God in Jerusalem or in the temple of the Samaritans.

Jesus answered that God had planned to bring salvation through the Jews, but he said the time had come when true worshipers need no longer go up to Jerusalem, for they might pray to God everywhere and worship him. "For God is a Spirit," he said, "and those who worship him in the right way must believe that he is a Spirit."

Then the woman said, "I know the Messiah is coming from God, and when he comes he will tell us everything."

"I am that Messiah," answered Jesus, and the woman looked in joy and wonder upon him. But at that moment the disciples returned from the city bringing food to eat, so she turned away and, leaving her water jug, ran back to tell her friends about the wonderful stranger whom she had met at the well.

The disciples wondered why Jesus would talk with a despised woman of the Samaritans; but they did not ask him any questions. They brought food to him, and when he refused to eat they urged him. Then he said to them, "I have food to eat which you know nothing about."

They asked each other, "Has someone brought food to him while we were away?"

But Jesus knew their questionings, so he said, "My meat is to do the will of my Father, who has sent me into the world."

When the woman reached the city she went into the streets and told the people about Jesus, the stranger who had understood all about her life. "He told me all the things that I ever did. Is not he the Messiah?" she asked. And the people decided to see this man for themselves, so they went with her to Jacob's well.

Jesus talked with the Samaritans about the things of God, and they invited him to stay in their city and teach them more of these wonderful truths. He spent two days in Sychar, teaching the people. Then he went on his way to Nazareth, leaving behind him some believers among the Samaritans.

Questions and Answers

1. Why did Jesus stop by the wayside well in Samaria? (He was tired.)

2. Why was the Samaritan woman surprised when Jesus asked her for a drink? (Because the Jews would not even speak to the Samaritans.)

3. Why did the woman believe that Jesus was a prophet? (Because he seemed to know about the wrong things she had done.)

4. Who did Jesus tell the woman that he was? (The Messiah for whom the people were looking.)

STORY 10

A Man of Great Faith

John 4:45-54

Many people who lived in the country of Galilee were eager to see Jesus. They had heard about his first miracle at Cana, where he turned water into wine, and they had heard also about his teachings and his miracles performed in Jerusalem during the Feast of the Passover. Now when he left Sychar and returned with his disciples to their country, the news of his coming spread rapidly from one city to another, and the Galilean people hoped he would come to their cities and perform miracles among them too.

But one man did not wait until Jesus should come to his home city before going out to see him. This man lived in Capernaum, a city that had been built on the shore of the Sea of Galilee. He was one of the rulers in that city, and he was called a nobleman. In the eyes of the poor who lived near his home he was a great man indeed; for he did not despise them, as did many of the rulers of the Jews.

Sorrow had come into the home of this nobleman, for his little son lay sick with a burning fever, and the doctors could not make him well. Hearing of Jesus, the

THE NOBLEMAN AND HIS SON

nobleman decided to seek this wonderful prophet and beg him to come to Capernaum to heal his child. So he left his home one night and hurried to Cana, where Jesus was.

When the nobleman found the place where Jesus was stopping, he called to see the wonderful prophet of Galilee. He told Jesus about his sick child lying at home at the point of death, and he asked Jesus to go with him to Capernaum to heal the child. But Jesus answered, "Unless you see signs and wonders you will not believe that I am sent of God."

The nobleman was very much in earnest. He cried out, "Sir, if you do not come down at once, my little son will be dead when we reach home."

Then Jesus spoke kindly to this distressed father. He said, "Return to your home without me, for your son will not die."

The nobleman believed Jesus' words and turned back to Capernaum. He did not fear any longer that death would snatch his dear child away from his loving care, for Jesus had said that the child should be well again. When he came near to Capernaum, his servants came to meet him with glad tidings. They said, "Your son is no longer sick."

"At what time," asked the nobleman, "did he begin to get well?"

And the servants replied, "His fever left him yesterday at the seventh hour of the day."

The ruler knew that Jesus had spoken to him at that very hour, and he believed surely that it was the power of this prophet that had saved the life of his child. Not only this nobleman, but all his household, too, believed in Jesus when they heard about the healing of the sick boy.

Questions and Answers

1. Why did the nobleman from Capernaum wish to see Jesus? (Because his son lay sick with a burning fever.)

2. Why did Jesus not go with the nobleman? (Perhaps Jesus wanted the people to know that he could heal without touching the person who was sick.)

3. What happened to the sick child while the father was talking with Jesus? (The fever left him.)

STORY 11

Jesus Speaks at Nazareth

Luke 4:16-32

A sad day had come for Nazareth, the city where Jesus had lived since his babyhood years. And this sad day had come on the Sabbath.

The Jews from different parts of the city were gathering in their house of worship, the synagogue. Among their number was Jesus, who had returned from his visit in Cana. Always while he lived in Nazareth he went every Sabbath Day to the services at the synagogue, where he heard God's words read from the books of the law and of the prophets.

Now, Jesus was no longer just an ordinary person among the other Jews of Nazareth, for they had heard about his teachings in other cities and they wished to hear for themselves what this son of the carpenter Joseph would say. So when the time came for the services to begin, Jesus stood up to read to the people, and the minister of the synagogue brought to him the book that the prophet Isaiah had written long years before. Jesus found where Isaiah wrote the prophecy concerning the Messiah, and he read Isaiah's prophecy to the people. These are some of the words he read:

"The Spirit of the Lord is upon me,
Because he hath anointed me to preach the gospel to the poor;
He has sent me to heal the brokenhearted,
To preach deliverance to the captives,
And recovering of sight to the blind,
To set at liberty them that are bruised,
To preach the acceptable year of the Lord."

After reading these words, Jesus closed the book, gave it back to the minister, and sat down. Then everyone in the synagogue looked at him, expecting to hear him speak; for the speaker in the synagogue always stood up to read God's words and sat down to explain the meaning of what he had read.

Among those who listened to Jesus that day were his neighbors who had known him nearly all his lifetime. Proud men they were, unwilling that the carpenter's son should teach them new truths. They had heard of the miracles that Jesus performed in Cana and in Capernaum, the city by the seashore. But they did not believe that Jesus was the promised King of the Jews. They knew he was only a poor man, and they did not respect him for being great and good.

But those proud men were surprised when they heard Jesus' words. They did not know he could speak so well. They did not know that he was the greatest teacher who had ever spoken to men. For a while they listened very carefully. Then Jesus told them that Isaiah's words were

JESUS IN THE SYNAGOGUE

fulfilled by his coming to preach the gospel to the poor and to do other wonderful things that Isaiah had promised. "How can this be true?" they asked of each other, "for is not this Joseph's son?"

Jesus knew they would not receive his words and believe them. He told them that no prophet was honored by his own people. And he reminded them of the time when Elijah the prophet ran away from Israel to hide in the home of a poor widow who lived in a heathen land. Because this poor widow cared for God's prophet, God took care of her. He also told them about the heathen leper, Naaman, who was healed by God's power when he obeyed Elisha's words, although many Israelites had leprosy and never were healed.

The proud men of Nazareth quickly objected to these words of Jesus, although they were true happenings among the Jews long before. They believed that Jesus was trying to show them how God cared for other people besides the Jews, and they did not like to hear such words. So they refused to listen longer to his teachings, and the service at the synagogue broke up in great disorder. The leading men ran to Jesus and took hold of him roughly and drew him outside their synagogue. Then a mob of angry people followed, wishing to see Jesus punished because he had spoken the truth to them.

This mob led Jesus to the top of the high hill upon which Nazareth was built, intending to throw him down upon the sharp rocks in the canyon below. But the time

JESUS PREACHING AT NAZARETH

had not yet come when Jesus should die for the sins of the people, and therefore they could not carry out their wicked intention. He simply walked quietly through the midst of the excited throng. No one seized hold of him again, and he left them and went away to live in Capernaum, the city by the Sea of Galilee.

The men of Nazareth did not know what a terrible deed they had tried to do that day; they did not know that their foolish pride had caused them to drive right out of their midst the gift which God had sent from heaven to earth. And because they refused to believe in Jesus as the one of whom Isaiah had written, they never received the gift of salvation which Jesus had brought to men.

Questions and Answers

1. How had Jesus spent every Sabbath while he lived in Nazareth? (He had always attended services at the synagogue.)
2. Why did the people of Nazareth become displeased with Jesus' teaching? (They were unwilling to think that God cared for people who were not Jews.)
3. What did they try to do? (To kill him.)
4. In what city did Jesus afterwards make his home? (Capernaum.)

STORY 12

Four Fishermen Leave Their Nets

Matt. 4:18-22; Mark 1:16-34; Luke 4:33—5:11

When Jesus returned from the Feast of the Passover at Jerusalem, his disciples were with him, you remember. But after coming into Galilee Jesus went to his home in Nazareth and the disciples returned to their homes in Capernaum.

After the proud men of Nazareth tried to kill Jesus, he left their city and went to live in Capernaum, too. Here he taught in the synagogue on the Sabbath Days, and the people of Capernaum were glad to listen to his words. He did not teach them as did their usual Jewish teachers, repeating the same words again and again each time he spoke, but always his words sounded new and just as if God were speaking to the people.

One morning Andrew and Simon were busy at work in their fishing boats on the Sea of Galilee when they saw Jesus walking along the shore. He called to them, and they left their boats and followed him. Farther along they saw two other fishermen in a ship mending their torn nets. These men were brothers, and their names were James and John. They were partners in the fishing business with Simon and Andrew. When they saw their partners following Jesus they looked up from their work, wondering where Simon and Andrew were going. Jesus called them also, and they left their ship at once in the care of their father and the servants who were helping mend the nets.

Taking these four fishermen with him, Jesus returned to the city. And on the next Sabbath Day they went with him into the synagogue, where many people had come to hear his words.

Among the crowd who had gathered that day in the synagogue was one man in whom Satan had put a very bad spirit. This bad spirit caused the man to cry aloud when he saw Jesus, and say, "Let us alone! What do we have to do with you, Jesus of Nazareth? I know you are the Holy One from God."

Jesus was not pleased to have a spirit of Satan speak to him like this. So he commanded the bad spirit to come out of the man. And the spirit threw the poor man on the floor before all the people, tearing him and crying with a wicked cry. But at Jesus' command the bad spirit had to leave the man; for Jesus has power over all the power of Satan, to cast out the evil spirits that come to dwell in people.

When those standing by saw what Jesus had done they were greatly astonished. Never before had they seen anyone with power to rebuke the evil spirits. They said to each other, "What thing is this? What new doctrine is this? Jesus even dares to command evil spirits and they must obey him!"

Quickly the news of this wonderful happening in the synagogue spread to every part of the city, and everybody became interested in the great teacher who had lately come to live among them. They were so glad he had come, and they wished to carry their suffering friends and loved ones to him that he might cure them of their sicknesses and diseases. So they began to plan how they might do this.

Jesus had gone with his disciples from the synagogue to the home of Simon and Andrew. When they arrived they heard that Simon's mother-in-law was lying sick with fever. They told Jesus about her, and brought him into the room where she lay suffering. Jesus came to her bedside, took hold of her hand, and lifted her up. At that very moment the fever departed and strength came into her body again. She rose from her bed and helped to prepare food for the disciples and their wonderful teacher.

At sunset the Sabbath Day closed for the Jews and they began their work again, for they never did any work on the Sabbath. When sunset came on this day of rest Simon and Andrew were surprised to see throngs of people coming toward their home. From every direction the people were coming, some with crippled friends leaning on their arms, and others with blind friends walking by their side. Others were carrying cots on which lay their sick children or other relatives. All of them were coming to ask Jesus to make their friends and loved ones well again.

What a busy time followed! Jesus was glad to help these poor sufferers and to make them well. He touched them, one by one, and they were healed. He even cast out many evil spirits from the people who had come, and he would not allow those spirits to cry out as the evil spirit had done in the synagogue.

Finally the last group of happy friends departed from the doorstep, and Jesus lay down to sleep in Simon's house. How very tired he must have been! But after sleeping only a few hours he rose up quietly and left the city. He found a place where he might be all alone to talk with his heavenly Father, for often he prayed earnestly to God for strength and help to do the great work that he had to do.

When daylight broke, people began coming again to Simon's home, asking for Jesus. But Jesus was not there. Simon and his friends began to search for Jesus, and they found him at his place of prayer. They told him about the anxious seekers who had come early to find him again, and Jesus said, "I must preach the kingdom of God in other cities also, for I am sent to do this great work." So the disciples went with him to visit other cities in Galilee, and Jesus taught in the synagogues of those cities and cast out evil spirits, as he had done in Capernaum. And many people believed in him.

JESUS AND THE FISHERMEN

After some time he returned again to Capernaum, and his disciples went back to their work as fishermen. But Jesus continued to teach the people who came to hear his words. One day he went out to the seaside where his disciples were washing their nets. Many people saw him leave the city, and they followed. Soon a great crowd gathered on the shore, eager to hear him preach. So Jesus asked permission to sit in Simon's ship and speak to the people who stood on the shore.

When Jesus finished speaking he told Simon to row out into the deep water and lower his net to catch some fish. Simon replied, "Master, we have fished all night and have caught nothing; however, if you wish we will try again." So they rowed away from the land and let down their nets once more. This time a great many fish were caught. Simon and Andrew could not draw them out of the water alone, for their net began to break with the weight of the many fish. They signaled for their partners, James and John, and the four men worked together. They had never seen so many fish in one net before. Soon the ship was filled, and they began to put fish into the second ship. Both ships began to sink with the weight of the fish and the men.

Now, the fishermen knew that Jesus had performed a miracle by causing so many fish to be in the net. Simon fell down at Jesus' knees and cried, "Leave me, O Lord! for I am a sinful man and am not worthy of all you have given to us here." But Jesus was not ready to leave

Simon. He answered, "Do not be afraid, for hereafter you shall catch men." And Simon understood from Jesus' words that he must leave his fishing business and follow the Master everywhere he went. When the fishers reached the shore they left their ships and walked with Jesus from one city to another, helping him and learning daily more and more about the kingdom of God.

Questions and Answers

1. Why did the four fishermen leave their boats and follow Jesus? (Because he called them to follow him.)

2. Who were these four men? (Andrew, Simon, James, and John.)

3. How did Jesus help the man who had a bad spirit? (He commanded the evil spirit to come out of the man.)

4. What did Jesus do for Simon's mother-in-law, who lay sick with fever? (He touched her hand, and the fever left her.)

5. Tell how Jesus helped his friends who had fished all night and caught nothing. (He told them where to find a good fishing place.)

A BUSY DAY AT CAPERNAUM

JESUS EATING WITH PUBLICANS

STORY 13

Matthew the Publican Becomes a Disciple

Matt. 9:9-13; Mark 2:14-17; Luke 5:27-32

In the land where Jesus lived there was among the Jews one class of people whom all other Jews despised. This class was the publicans, or taxgatherers, who worked for the Roman government.

The Jews hated the Roman government because they wished to be an independent nation, having a Jewish ruler over them. For this reason they were eagerly awaiting the time when the kingdom of God should come. They believed the kingdom of God would be set up in their country and would be like the kingdom over which David ruled. And they expected to become the greatest people in all the world then. They hated any Jew who was friendly with the Roman government, because they thought he was not true to his own nation.

For many years the Jews had believed God would send them a king who would deliver them from the rule of stronger nations. They did not understand when the prophets taught of Jesus' coming to earth that he would come to free them from their greatest enemy, Satan. They seemed to forget that they needed freedom from sin's bondage more than they needed freedom from the rule of the heathen kings.

The Jews who were more friendly toward the Romans, and who worked for the Roman government, were called publicans. They took the tax money from the Jews, which the ruler at Rome demanded of them. And often they took more money than was called for by the Roman ruler. This extra money, which they really stole from the people, they kept for themselves, and so became very rich. The people hated them, and called them sinners.

Not all the publicans robbed the people by asking too much tax money from them. But because many of them did this, the people called every publican a sinner.

One day while Jesus was passing along a street in the city of Capernaum he saw a man named Matthew sitting at a publican's table, taking the tax money from the people. Although Matthew was a despised publican, Jesus saw his heart and he knew Matthew would make a good disciple. He called this publican to follow him, and Matthew gladly left his money table and obeyed.

Matthew was also called Levi, for the Jews sometimes had two names. And after he began to follow Jesus he remembered his friends of other days. He believed they, too, would be glad to see Jesus and to hear his words. So Matthew prepared a great feast and invited to it many of his publican friends, as well as other people whom the proud Jews despised and called sinners. He also brought Jesus and the other disciples to the feast.

The scribes and Pharisees also came to Matthew's house that day, though they had not been invited. They stood about in the courtyard or even in the large dining hall, looking on and talking to each other about what they saw. This was not so rude as it seems, for this was a custom among those people, and Matthew was not at all surprised when they came.

These onlookers began to find fault when they saw Jesus sitting among the publicans and sinners. They felt themselves too good to keep company with despised people, and they were surprised that Jesus should eat with Matthew and his friends. So they called Jesus' disciples aside and asked, "How is it that your Master eats and drinks with publicans and sinners?"

Jesus heard the questioning of these faultfinders, and he said to them, "It is not well people who need to call for the services of a doctor, but people who are sick. And so I have not come to call righteous people, but I have come to call sinners to repent."

Matthew the publican became a very useful man for God. It was he who wrote the "Gospel of Matthew."

Questions and Answers

1. Who were the publicans? (They were Jews who worked for the Roman government.)

2. What work was Matthew doing when Jesus called him to be a disciple? (He was collecting tax money from the people.)

3. Why did Matthew prepare a great feast at his house? (He wanted his friends to meet Jesus.)

4. What part of the Bible did Matthew the publican write? (He wrote the first book in the New Testament, the Gospel of Matthew.)

JESUS HELPING A CRIPPLED MAN

STORY 14

Jesus Heals a Crippled Man

Matt. 12:1-8; Mark 2:23-28; Luke 6:1-5; John 5:1-18

Not far from the Temple in Jerusalem was a pool called Bethesda. At certain times the water in this pool was made to bubble on the surface.

Many sick people, and cripples, and blind persons came to the pool and waited long for the water to move. Five porches were built beside the pool where these afflicted people might rest in the shade and wait for a chance to be cured by bathing in the troubled waters.

One Sabbath Day while Jesus was in Jerusalem he walked through the porches beside the pool. And there he saw the afflicted people who had come for healing. How many there were we do not know. Lying on a mat near the edge of a porch was a man who had not walked for nearly forty years. What a pitiful sight he was! Jesus knew how long the poor man had been crippled, although no one told him. He stopped by the man, and asked gently, "Would you like to be made well?"

Perhaps the cripple thought this a strange question. He answered, "Sir, I have no one to help me when the water moves, and before I can crawl down someone else steps in."

Jesus said, "Rise up, take your bed and walk!" The surprised man felt strength pouring into his weakened body, and he sprang to his feet. Then he rolled up the mat, and taking it in his arms started toward his home. How happy he felt! But he could not thank Jesus for he had disappeared in the crowd.

Some religious Jews saw him carrying his bed. Because they believed it was sinful to carry burdens on the Sabbath Day, they stopped him and asked why he was carrying his bed. He answered, "I was lying a cripple by the pool when a stranger came to me and told me to rise up and take my bed and walk away with it."

"Who is this stranger?" they demanded, for they were angry to think that anyone should break one of the laws they kept on the Sabbath. But the poor man did not know who Jesus was, so he could not tell.

Not long afterwards Jesus found the man in the Temple, worshiping God. Jesus told him to sin no more, lest something worse than his long affliction should come upon him. Then the man knew who Jesus was, and he ran out to tell the people about who had made him well.

The Jews were angry because Jesus had healed the poor man on the Sabbath Day. They did not care for the poor sufferer so much as they cared for their own pretenses to be righteous. They believed it was wrong to do even such a good work as healing the sick on the Sabbath. But Jesus told them that his Father worked on the Sabbath, and so did he. Then they were more angry than ever because he said that God was his Father. They wished to kill him.

After this time the Pharisees became enemies of Jesus. They often followed him just to find fault. One Sabbath Day while he was walking with his disciples through a field of corn, the disciples picked off some of the kernels to eat, because they were hungry. The Pharisees were near by, and seeing what the disciples had done they came to Jesus to find fault. They said, "Your disciples are breaking the Sabbath laws, for they are gathering food to eat."

Jesus told the Pharisees that God was not pleased with their regard of the Sabbath law that would not allow a person to do even what is right. He reminded them of the time when David ate from the Temple the bread that belonged only to the priests. God knew David and his men were hungry, so he did not punish David for this act. He told the Pharisees that the priests and the Levites work every Sabbath, when they offer the morning and the evening sacrifices. And he said, "The Son of Man is Lord even of the Sabbath Day."

Questions and Answers

1. Why did many afflicted people gather at the pool called Bethesda? (They came hoping to be healed.)
2. How long had one man been crippled? (Nearly forty years.)
3. What did Jesus tell this man to do? (Rise, take up his bed, and walk.)
4. What did Jesus' enemies say about this miracle? (They were angry because Jesus had healed on the Sabbath.)

STORY 15

Jesus Chooses the Twelve

Matt. 10:2-4; Mark 3:13-19; Luke 6:12-16

Many people besides the fishermen and Philip and Nathanael and Matthew followed Jesus. Jesus' teachings were so wonderful that others wished to be learners, or disciples, of him, and so they followed in his company from one place to another.

But the time came when Jesus wished to choose from among this company twelve men whom he could prepare to help in his great work. These men he wished to send out to places where he never yet had been, and have them preach to the people in those places about the kingdom of God.

Although Jesus could see the hearts of all men, yet he felt that he needed help from God to know which of his followers he should choose to be among his twelve helpers. One night he went away quietly and climbed up the slope of a mountain, where no one would be near to disturb him. There he knelt down to pray, and all night he prayed to God for help and wisdom and strength to do his work.

When morning light returned, Jesus was ready to choose his helpers, so he left his place of prayer and

JESUS CHOOSING DISCIPLES

JESUS TEACHING

joined the company of disciples who were waiting in the valley for his coming. From them he chose Simon, whom he called Peter, and Andrew, the brother who first brought Simon to Jesus. Then he chose James and John, the fishermen who had been partners with Simon and Andrew at the seaside. Afterwards he chose Matthew, the publican, and Philip and Nathanael, of Capernaum, and Thomas, and another James, who was the son of Alphaeus, and another Simon, also called Zelotes, then Judas the brother of James, and last of all Judas Iscariot, who finally sold his Lord.

To these twelve men Jesus gave power to cure diseases and to cast out devils. He also appointed them to preach the kingdom of God. And he called them his apostles, which means "those who are sent out," because he sent them out to preach to other men.

Of these twelve apostles we read the most about Simon Peter, James, John, Andrew, Matthew, Philip, and Thomas. Little mention is made of the others, except of Judas Iscariot, who near the end of Jesus' ministry became untrue and betrayed Jesus.

Questions and Answers

1. Why did Jesus choose twelve men to be his disciples? (He wished to train them to become helpers in his great work.)
2. What did Jesus do just before this important event? (He spent the night on a mountain in prayer to God.)
3. Which of these twelve men proved unworthy of Jesus' confidence? (Judas Iscariot.)
4. What did Jesus send these men out to do? (To preach the gospel and to heal the sick.)

STORY 16

The Sermon on the Mountainside

Matthew 5—7; Luke 6:17-49

After Jesus had chosen his twelve apostles, who were still called disciples, he took them apart from the multitude to teach them how to do his great work. Up the side of the mountain they went together, and there Jesus sat down. His disciples stood near and he spoke to them. Other people also climbed the mountain to listen to the great sermon Jesus preached that day.

In the beginning of his sermon Jesus said: "Blessed are the poor in spirit: for theirs is the kingdom of heaven." Perhaps he had been thinking about the proud spirits of the scribes and Pharisees. He knew that proud spirits will never receive his words and learn how to enter the kingdom of God. But people who are humble and who do not believe themselves to be righteous without God's help he called poor in spirit, and he said they are blessed because to them shall be given the kingdom of God, for which all Jews were seeking.

He also said: "Blessed are they that mourn: for they shall be comforted." These words sounded strange to the listeners, for they had never thought that blessings belonged to those who are grieving because of troubles and sorrows. They did not realize how God loves to comfort the weary and sad.

"Blessed are the meek," said Jesus next, "for they shall inherit the earth." By these words he meant that gentle people who do not lose their temper and allow thoughts of discontent to fill their minds will be happy and will enjoy the blessings God gives to all men.

Then Jesus said, "Blessed are they which do hunger and thirst after righteousness: for they shall be filled." Perhaps he was thinking again of the proud Pharisees, who believed they were righteous in themselves and therefore did not need to repent of their sins and seek the righteousness of God. Only those are blessed with God's righteousness who long for it as earnestly as they wish for food and drink to satisfy their appetites.

"Blessed are they who show mercy to others," said Jesus, "for mercy shall be shown to them. And blessed are they who have pure hearts, for they shall see God. And blessed are they who make peace among men, for they shall be called the children of God." These words the disciples understood; for they knew God will surely bless people who show mercy, and people who will not allow sin to enter their hearts, and people who bring peace where trouble is.

Then Jesus said, "Blessed are they who are persecuted for the sake of righteousness; for theirs is the kingdom of heaven." These words sounded strange, for people who are persecuted are greatly troubled; and the disciples may have wondered how the kingdom of God could belong to them when trouble was filling their lives. But afterwards they learned how people who are being persecuted for the sake of righteousness can be blessed as citizens of the kingdom of heaven. And after Jesus had been crucified and had risen from the dead, they themselves learned what it means to be persecuted for the sake of righteousness. Jesus said that those who are so persecuted should rejoice and be very glad, because there is a great reward awaiting them in heaven.

In this wonderful sermon Jesus told the people how Christians should live. He taught them how Christians should pray. He taught them how they should treat their enemies and their friends. He told them about God's love and care for those who trust him.

At the close of his long sermon, Jesus said: "Those who hear my words and do them are like the man who builds his house on a foundation of rock. When the winds blow and the rain falls fast, that foundation of rock will stand firm, and the house will not fall. But those who hear my words and do not obey them are like the man who builds his house on a foundation of sand. When the winds blow and the rain falls fast, that sandy foundation will be washed out from beneath the building, and the house will fall."

Jesus meant by these words that people who hear and obey his teachings will be saved. And when the storm of the Judgment Day comes they will be safe from harm. But people who hear his teachings and refuse to obey them will not be safe when the storm of the Judgment Day comes upon them.

When Jesus ended his sermon, the people looked at each other in surprise. They knew his teachings were more wonderful than the teachings of Moses and of the scribes and Pharisees. They wondered who could obey such commands as these: "Love your enemies"; "Pray for them who treat you wrongly"; "Do good to them who hate you." But they knew that Jesus' words sounded as though they were the words of God, and by and by many of them learned that even the hardest commands could be obeyed by those who truly love the Lord.

Questions and Answers

1. To what place did Jesus take his twelve apostles to teach them his doctrine? (He took them to a quiet place on a mountainside.)

2. Who did Jesus say were blessed? (The poor, the sorrowing, the meek, the merciful, the pure in heart, and others.)

3. Whom did Jesus say those who hear his words and obey them are like? (They are like the man who builds his house on a foundation of rock.)

JESUS HEALING A LEPER

STORY 17

Jesus Heals a Leper

Matt. 8:1-4; Mark 1:40-45; Luke 5:12-16

When Jesus and his twelve disciples came down from the mountain, a great multitude of people followed them. These people had come from cities and villages in Galilee, from Jerusalem, and from country places in Judea.

Near this great multitude stood one poor man who had heard of Jesus' power to work miracles. He needed to have a miracle performed in his body for he had leprosy. He was not allowed to live among his friends and relatives, or anyone else, for fear they might become lepers also.

When the poor leper saw Jesus and his disciples coming down the mountainside, he thought, "I wonder if this Jesus will heal me." He decided to try him. Running to Jesus, he knelt down on the ground at Jesus' feet, worshiping him. Then he said, "If you are willing, I know you can make me well from this terrible leprosy."

Jesus looked on the poor man kneeling before him, and great pity filled his heart. He knew how this man was dying by inches of the dreaded leprosy, which no doctors could cure. He knew about the unhappy days this poor man spent away from his own home and loved ones, and how everyone was afraid to be near him.

Jesus was not afraid to touch the poor leper. He reached out his hand kindly, and said, "I am willing; you may be healed now." And at that moment the leprosy left the man's body and new skin came upon his flesh.

The man sprang quickly to his feet, and the weary look vanished from his eyes. Now he was well! How thankful he felt! No doubt the great change seemed too good to believe. But he saw how the leprosy was gone, and he knew Jesus had healed him.

In the Jewish law lepers were commanded to offer sacrifices of thanksgiving to God when their leprosy was healed. Jesus reminded the man of this command and told him to go to the priests in Jerusalem and make an offering to God.

Soon the news of this great miracle spread over the countryside, and everyone was talking about it. The poor man had been so glad that he had told his friends what Jesus had done for him. His friends told their friends, and so the news spread far and wide. Many people left their homes and rushed into the country to see the wonderful person.

Questions and Answers

1. Why were leprous persons not permitted to come near to other people? (Leprosy is contagious.)
2. As this leper knelt in the dust of the roadside, what did he tell Jesus? ("If you are willing, I know you can make me well.")
3. Why was Jesus not afraid to touch the leper? (Because he had power to overcome all kinds of diseases.)
4. What did Jesus tell the man to do after he was healed? (To go to the priests in Jerusalem and make an offering to God.)

STORY 18

A Roman Captain Shows Great Faith in Jesus

Matt. 8:5-13; Luke 7:1-10

After healing the leper Jesus returned with his disciples to Capernaum, where he had healed so many sick people at the close of one Sabbath Day. News of his coming reached the city before he arrived, and his friends were glad to hear that he would be with them.

Other people besides those who knew him were glad to hear of his coming. One of them was a Roman, called by the Jews a "Gentile," because he did not belong to the Jewish nation, or race. All people who are not Jews are called Gentiles, and this Gentile was captain of a band of one hundred Roman soldiers. He was called a centurion by those people.

This captain, or centurion, was friendly toward the Jews. He treated them kindly, never roughly. He even built for them a synagogue, perhaps the very one in which Jesus had often taught the people on the Sabbath Days. Because of his kindness the Jews respected him.

One day a servant of the centurion became sick. On the next day he grew worse, and soon it seemed that he could not live much longer. The centurion loved this

JESUS WITH THE ROMAN CENTURION

servant and grieved because he was ill. Then news came that Jesus had returned to Capernaum.

Now, the centurion had heard about the sick people whom Jesus had cured and about the evil spirits which Jesus had driven out of people's hearts. He knew Jesus could heal his servant, but he felt too unworthy to go to Jesus and ask him to do this. He was a Roman, and he knew that Jesus was a Jew. Perhaps he thought Jesus might not be willing to listen to the request of a man who belonged to another nation. He knew about the race pride of the Jews, and how the religious Pharisees and the scribes despised the Gentile Romans. He may have feared that Jesus would not be quite willing to heal his servant because he was a Gentile. But he loved his servant very dearly, and he was willing to try to have Jesus come and heal him. So he called for the Jewish teachers in the synagogue which he had built, and told them to go to Jesus and ask him to heal the sick man.

When these Jewish teachers, or elders, came to Jesus they told him about the centurion's desire that he would come and heal the servant. They told him also about the kindness of this Roman captain, and how he had built their synagogue. "He is a worthy man," they said, "for he loves our nation." Jesus went with them.

As they were nearing the centurion's home they saw some men coming to meet them. These men were friends of the centurion, whom he had sent to tell Jesus that he need not come into the house to heal the sick man. The centurion did not feel worthy to have such a great person as Jesus enter under the roof of his house, and he felt himself too unworthy to go out to meet Jesus. So he had sent his friends to carry his message to Jesus. And this was the message: "Lord, do not trouble yourself to come into my house, for I am not worthy to receive so great a man as you are. Just speak the word, and my servant will be made well. I know you have power to command sickness to depart, just as I have power to command my soldiers to obey me."

When Jesus heard these words he was greatly pleased. There was a crowd of curious people following, hoping to see another miracle. He turned about and said to them, "Nowhere among the Jews have I found such great faith in me as this Gentile captain has shown." Then he told the friends of the centurion that the servant would be made well.

When they returned to the house they found the servant healed. And they saw how great was the power of Jesus to heal the sick.

Questions and Answers

1. What kindness had the Roman captain shown toward the Jews? (He had built them a synagogue.)

2. Why was he glad when he heard that Jesus had returned to Capernaum? (He hoped that Jesus would heal his sick servant.)

3. Whom did he send to speak to Jesus about coming to heal his servant? (Some Jewish elders, or teachers in the synagogue.)

4. Why did the captain send friends to tell Jesus he need not bother to come to his house to heal the sick servant? (Because he believed Jesus had power to heal by speaking the word only.)

STORY 19

Four Men Tear Up a Roof

Matt. 9:2-8; Mark 2:1-12; Luke 5:18-26

Wherever Jesus went, crowds followed him. In the streets, or even in the homes of Capernaum, many people gathered when they knew he was present. Some of these people were his friends, others were merely persons curious to hear him speak and to see him perform some miracle. Others followed for the purpose of finding fault with him.

One day while Jesus was in Capernaum so many people came to the house where he was staying that they left no room for others to enter. Among them, as usual, were his disciples and friends, the curiosity seekers, and the faultfinders. These faultfinders were scribes and Pharisees who had come from far-off places to hear him. They had heard many reports about his wonderful teachings, and they wished to hear him for themselves. As he talked, they sat near by, watching every move he made.

Into that crowded room sick people had been brought, and Jesus healed them all. While he was preaching about the kingdom of God the listeners were surprised to hear a scrambling overhead. Presently the roof began to part,

THE MAN WITH FOUR FRIENDS

and the people saw a queer-looking object being lowered from the ceiling. Soon they recognized the form of a crippled man lying on a bed.

On the roof were the four friends of this crippled man. They had tried to bring him to Jesus, but when they had carried him as far as the door they saw that it would not be possible to push through the crowd with their burden. Yet they were determined to bring this suffering man to the great Healer. The man was not able to move himself about, and day after day he had lain weak and helpless upon his bed because of the disease.

When the crowd had refused to make way for them to pass, the four friends carried the man up on the flat roof of the house. They tore up the roof tiling and saw where Jesus stood. This done, they tied ropes about the bed on which the man lay and lowered the bed very carefully into the room, before Jesus.

Of course the service was interrupted when the sick man was being lowered by the ropes from the roof. The onlookers wondered what Jesus would do. Perhaps some of them knew this sick man. They were all surprised when they heard Jesus say to him, "Son, be of good cheer, for your sins are forgiven."

The look of pain left the sick man's face, and a happy smile came instead. But the astonished people were not watching him. They were looking in surprise at the one who had dared to say, "Your sins are forgiven." They knew God had power to forgive sins, but they did not

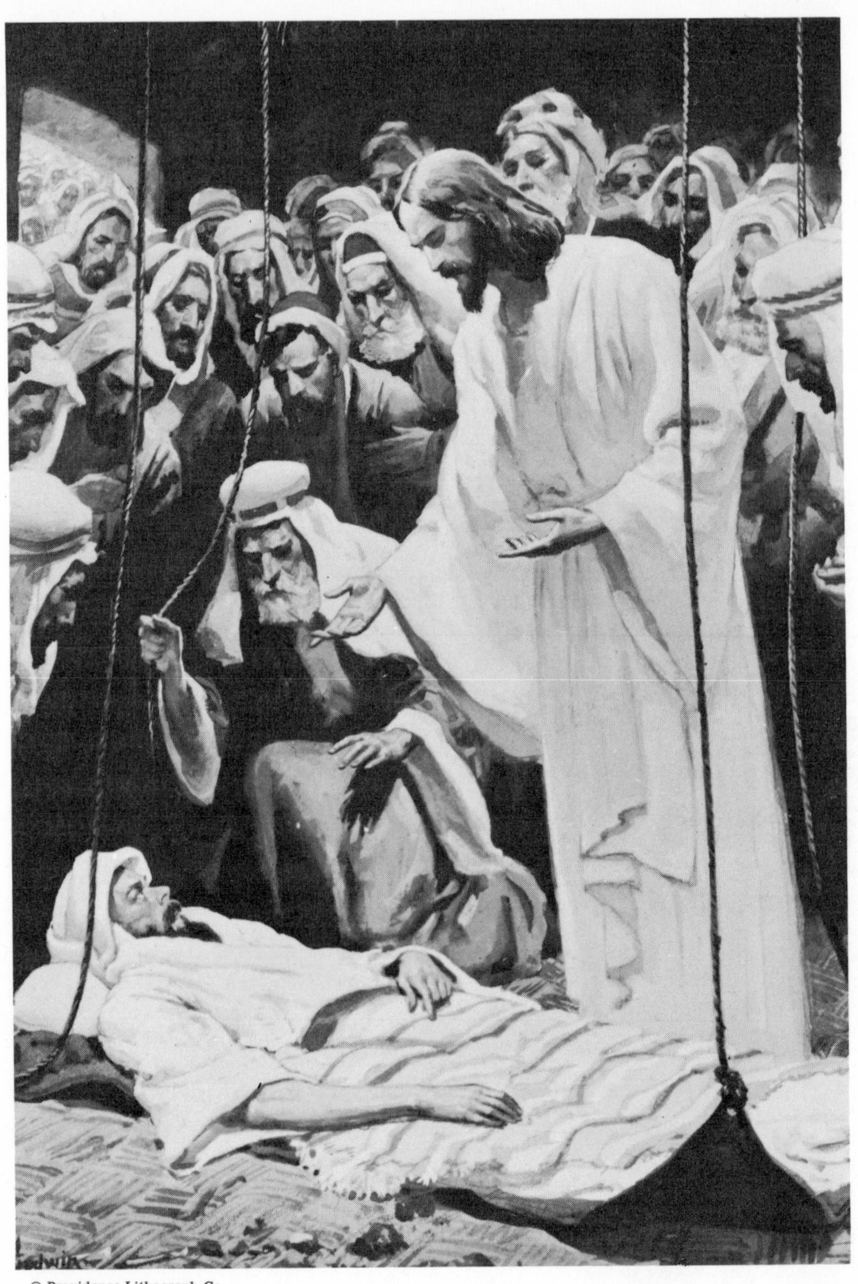

THE MAN LET DOWN THOUGH THE ROOF

know that Jesus was the Son of God. The faultfinders began to say in their hearts, "Who is this who pretends to forgive sins? None except God can do that!"

Jesus knew their thoughts, and he said, "Why do you think evil of me in your hearts? Is it easier to tell the man that his sins are forgiven, or to tell him to rise up from his bed and walk? But that you may know I have power on earth to forgive sins too [Jesus turned to the helpless man lying on the couch before him and said], Arise, take up your bed, and return to your own house."

Immediately the stiffness departed from the sick man's limbs, and strength came into his body. Then he rose in the presence of all the people, rolled up the couch, or mat, upon which he had lain for many days, and lifted it up on his shoulders, just as well men carried their beds in that country. The surprised people made way for him, and he walked out through the crowd into the street to join his happy friends.

Great fear came upon the people in that crowded house. They glorified God, and said to each other as they hurried home, "Surely we have seen strange things today!"

Questions and Answers

1. What strange thing happened while Jesus was teaching in a house in Capernaum? (Through a hole in the roof, a crippled man was lowered in the presence of Jesus.)
2. Why had the four men brought their crippled friend to Jesus in this queer way? (They could not pass through the crowd with him.)
3. How did Jesus encourage the poor man's faith? (He said, "Son, be of good cheer, for your sins are forgiven.")

JESUS RAISING THE WIDOW'S SON

STORY 20

A Widow's Sorrow Is Changed into Joy

Luke 7:11-17

In the city of Nain, in Galilee, lived a woman who was a widow. She had only one child, a youth entering manhood. She often looked at him proudly and thought the time would soon come when he could provide for her needs as well as for his own. Then one day the young man fell sick.

This was a sad time for the widow, and day after day she watched at the bedside of her son, hoping to see a change for the better. Tenderly she nursed him; but in spite of all her loving care he grew worse. One day he died.

Now the widow's home was broken up, for both her husband and her son were dead. How unhappy she felt! Her neighbors and friends came in to weep with her and to plan for the funeral. They wrapped long strips of linen cloth around the lifeless body and placed it on a frame, called a bier. Then they took up the bier and started with it to the burial place outside the city gate.

Many people followed the bier, and the mourners wept aloud as the procession moved slowly toward the burial place. Outside the gate they suddenly stopped. Everybody wondered what had happened. Then they saw a great crowd coming toward them, and walking in front of the crowd was Jesus with his twelve disciples.

When Jesus saw the grief of the widow he was touched with pity for her. He knew how deep was her sorrow, and he wished to help. He spoke kindly to her, "Do not weep." Then he stepped up to the bier, and the men who carried it looked at him. They were astonished when they heard him speak to the lifeless form that was lying so cold and helpless. At Jesus' words, "Young man, I tell you to arise!" they saw the lifeless body rise to a sitting position, and they heard the voice which death had stilled speak to them again. What a glad surprise this was! Quickly they unwrapped the long strips of linen cloth from the young man's body, and Jesus took him to his mother.

Now the cries of mourning ceased, and a great silence fell over the people. They could hardly believe their own eyes. But soon they were convinced that Jesus had raised the dead young man to life again, and they began to rejoice. "A great prophet is come among us!" they exclaimed with delight. Others cried, "Surely God has visited his people!"

News of this great miracle quickly spread through the country and traveled far and wide. Even John the Baptist, shut up in the dreary prison where Herod had placed him, heard what Jesus had done. He longed to see and to know more about these things, so he asked two of his disciples who visited him at the prison if they would not go to Jesus and find out whether Jesus was really the Savior whom God had promised to send.

The men hurried to Jesus with John's question, and while they waited for an answer many suffering people crowded close to the place where they stood, and begged for healing. One by one Jesus healed them and sent them away. Then he turned to the inquirers who had come from John's lonely prison, and said, "Go back, and tell John what you have seen; how the blind see, the lame walk, the deaf hear, the lepers are cured, the dead are raised to life, the evil spirits are cast out, and to the poor people the glad news of the kingdom is preached."

The men took this message back to John, and his heart was glad to hear about the wonderful workings of Jesus. Not long after this time Herod commanded that John should be killed, and his friends came and told Jesus what Herod had done.

Questions and Answers

1. Who stopped a funeral procession outside the city of Nain? (Jesus.)

2. How did Jesus show his great love and power there? (He made the dead alive, so that he could care for his mother, who was a widow.)

3. Why did John the Baptist send two friends to speak to Jesus? (He was shut up in prison and could not visit Jesus.)

4. What was the sad end of John the Baptist? (He was beheaded at the command of Herod, who had shut him up in prison.)

STORY 21

Jesus at the Home of a Pharisee

Luke 7:36-50

In one of the cities of Galilee where Jesus was teaching the people, a Pharisee named Simon came to hear him. Like many of the other Pharisees, Simon tried to find fault with Jesus. Because he could neither see nor hear anything to criticize in Jesus, he decided to ask this teacher to take dinner at his house. There he would watch him closely and possibly find something that would be wrong.

So Simon the Pharisee asked Jesus to come to his house one day, and Jesus went with him. Other people went, too; some who were invited and some who were not. And they all came into the dining hall, where the food was placed on the table. Around this table the guests were given room, while the uninvited persons stood back, looking on.

Jesus and the other guests did not sit on chairs about the table, but lay on couches with their heads near the table and their feet away from it. While they were eating, another uninvited person came into the dining hall. This person was a woman. Looking about, she saw Jesus, and at once she hurried to kneel at his feet. Then she wept tears of sorrow for her many sins, and the tears fell upon Jesus' feet. She dried his feet with her hair, and kissed them. Afterwards she broke a beautiful box of costly perfume and anointed his feet by pouring the perfume upon them.

Simon, the Pharisee, knew this woman, who was a great sinner. He had heard many things about her that were not good. He was surprised when he saw that Jesus allowed her to weep at his feet and to anoint them with sweet perfume. He said in his heart, "If Jesus were a prophet he would not allow this woman to come near him. He would know that she is a wretched sinner, unfit to be in his presence."

Jesus knew all about this sinful woman, and he also knew about Simon's thoughts. He looked at the proud Pharisee and said, "Simon, I have something to tell you."

Simon answered very politely, "Master, what is it?" Then Jesus told him this story:

"There was a certain rich man who had lent money to two poor men. To one man he lent a great sum of money, and to the second man he lent only a small amount. When the time came to repay the loan, neither of the two men could pay back the money they had borrowed. In their distress they came to the rich man, and he freely forgave them both. Which of these two men loved the rich man the more?"

"I suppose," answered Simon, "that the man whom he forgave the bigger debt loved him the more."

"You have answered rightly," said Jesus. Then he turned to the sinful woman still weeping at his feet, and said, "Simon, when I came into your home you did not treat me like an honored guest. You did not give me water to wash the dust from my feet; but this woman has washed my feet with her tears and has dried them with the hair of her head. You did not give me a kiss of welcome; but this woman has kissed my feet. You did not anoint my head with oil, as you anoint the heads of your friends who come as guests into your home; but this woman has poured costly ointment upon my feet. Wherefore I tell you that her sins, which were many, are forgiven; for she has loved much. But those love little who have little forgiven them."

Jesus then told the woman that her sins were forgiven, that her faith had brought forgiveness, and she should go home in peace. This woman was sorry because she had done wrong, and Jesus forgave the wrong which she had done.

Questions and Answers

1. Why did Simon the Pharisee ask Jesus to dine at his home? (He wanted to watch him closely and find some fault in him.)
2. Who washed Jesus' feet with tears that day? (A sinful woman.)
3. What did the proud Pharisee think of Jesus when he let the woman touch his feet? (He thought that if Jesus were a prophet he would not allow her to touch him.)
4. How did Jesus rebuke Simon for his wrong thoughts? (By telling him a story and then asking him questions.)
5. How did he show his pity to the sinful woman? (By forgiving her sins and sending her home in peace.)

THE WOMAN AND THE PERFUME

THE SOWER IN A FIELD

STORY 22

Story Sermons by the Sea

Matt. 13:1-53; Mark 4:1-34

One day Jesus went out of Capernaum with his disciples and walked by the seaside. Great crowds followed along the beach; for they thought he might be going away from their city again, and they wished to go with him. They pressed so close behind that Jesus stepped into a boat at the water's edge and sat down to teach them, while they stood listening on the shore.

Jesus began to teach them by parables. These parables were short stories which he told to show them truths of the gospel. While he sat in the boat he told them some parables. The first one was about the man who went out to scatter seeds in his field. Jesus called him a sower. And here is the story:

"One day a sower went out to the field with a bag of grain and began to scatter the seeds upon the ground. The breeze caught each handful he threw while walking to and fro, and helped to scatter the grain. But some of the seeds blew upon the roadside. The birds flying overhead saw them lying uncovered on the hard ground, so they flew down and ate them. Other seeds fell upon stony places, where the soil was so shallow they could take no deep root, and soon after they had sprouted and begun to grow they withered. Other seeds fell in thorny places, and the thorns grew so fast that they choked out the good seed, and it died.

"But not all the seed was wasted; some of it fell into good ground, and there it sprouted and sent its roots down deep into the rich soil. By and by it grew up into stalks of grain that yielded many times more seeds than were first scattered on the ground."

The disciples wondered what this story might mean. They did not know why Jesus was telling stories instead of preaching sermons that the people could understand. They asked Jesus, "Why are you teaching the people with these parables?"

Jesus answered, "Because I know you will seek to understand the meaning of them, for it is given to you to know the meaning of the deep truths of the kingdom of heaven. Others who hear the stories will not seek to understand the meaning of them, for they are not careful to prepare their hearts to receive the forgiveness of their sins. The prophet Isaiah spoke of them when he said, 'By hearing ye shall hear and not understand; and seeing ye shall see and not know.' Their eyes are closed, so they cannot see the salvation God has sent into the world; and their ears are stopped, so they cannot hear the good news of salvation and receive it into their hearts. But blessed are your eyes, for they see; and blessed are your ears, for they hear."

Then Jesus explained to the disciples the meaning of the story about the sower and his seed.

"The sower," he said, "is the one who speaks the word of God, and the different kinds of soil are the different conditions of the hearts of people who hear the word of God spoken. Those who hear the word but do not seek to understand it, are like the roadside by which the seeds fell. Just as the birds flew down and ate those seeds, so the evil one comes by and causes those people to forget the truths they have heard from God's word.

"Those who gladly hear the word of God, but do not continue to obey it, are like the stony places, where the seeds fell but could not grow because they could not take deep roots in the stony soil.

"Those who hear and receive the word of God into their hearts, but afterwards allow cares and troubles or riches and pleasures to crowd out the good truths, are like the soil where thorns sprang up and choked out the good seed.

"But those who hear and who obey the words of God are like the good ground, where some of the seeds fell and sprouted and grew into stalks that bore much grain."

Afterwards Jesus told another story to the people. This time he said: "The kingdom of heaven is like a man who sowed good seeds in his field; but while men slept an enemy came to the field and scattered bad seeds everywhere. These bad seeds are called tares. By and by the good seeds and the bad seeds both began to grow. And after they became stalks, and heads of grain appeared, the servants of the man came to him and asked, 'Did you not sow good seeds in your field? How then are these tares growing everywhere beside the stalks of wheat?' The man answered, 'An enemy has sown the tares.' Then the servants asked, 'Shall we gather out the tares?' but the master said, 'Wait until the time for harvest, lest while you pull up the tares you also pull up stalks of wheat. When all are ripened together, I will send reapers to gather out the tares first and tie them into bundles to be thrown into the fire. Then they will gather the wheat and put it into my barn.' "

The third story Jesus told was about a grain of mustard seed. He said the kingdom of heaven is like such a tiny grain, which, after it was sown, quickly grew into a bush so large that even the birds could sit in the branches of it.

Then he said, "The kingdom of heaven is also like leaven, or yeast, which a woman put into her dough when she was mixing bread. The yeast soon worked through all the dough and caused it to rise light and make good bread." Perhaps the women who heard this story wondered how the kingdom of heaven could really be like yeast.

When Jesus finished all his stories he sent the people away, and afterwards he left the boat and returned to the city. Then the disciples asked him to explain the meaning of the story about the tares. Jesus said: "The good seed are the people of God; the field is the world; and the man who sowed the good seed is the Son of Man. The bad seed, or tares, are the people of the wicked one, and the enemy is Satan. The harvest is the end of the world, and the reapers are the angels. Just as the tares are gathered in bundles and thrown into the fire, so the wicked people will be separated from the good people at the end of the world. Then the good people will shine as brightly as the sun in the kingdom of God, their Father."

Questions and Answers

1. What is a parable? (A short story which teaches a lesson.)
2. Name four of Jesus' parables. (The Sower, the Wheat and the Tares, the Mustard Seed, and the Leaven.)
3. To whom did Jesus explain his parables? (The disciples.)
4. Tell the parable of the sower. (The good seed which he sowed fell on different kinds of soil and yielded accordingly.)

STORY 23

The Flooded Ship That Did Not Sink

Matt. 8:23-34; Mark 4:35-41

One stormy night a little ship tossed about on the angry waters of the Sea of Galilee. It had sailed far from the shore when the storm broke upon it, and the sailors feared they might never see land again. With all their strength they pulled the oars; but the great waves dashed the ship helplessly about, threatening to destroy it.

Several of the sailors in that company had seen the rage of the sea at other times when storms swept over it. They knew the fearful power of such a storm. They knew how helpless they were in the grasp of this tempest. While they were wondering what to do, a great wave broke over the side of the ship, flooding it with water. Now they believed that they would drown.

These frightened sailors were the disciples of Jesus, and they were trying to take their master across the Sea of Galilee. Darkness had come upon them, and with the darkness of night the fearful storm broke. Jesus, tired from his labors during the day, had lain down to rest and had fallen fast asleep. He did not know about the raging tempest, which threatened to destroy the ship

JESUS STILLING THE STORM

and its passengers. He did not know about the fright of his disciples as they battled with the storm.

But when the great wave broke over the ship, the disciples remembered Jesus, lying asleep. They rushed to him and cried out, "Master, do you not care that we perish?"

Jesus aroused from his sleep, opened his eyes, and looked into their frightened faces. Seeing their alarm he arose to his feet and asked, "Why are you so fearful? Why do you have no faith?" Then he spoke to the wind, simply telling it to be still. And at the sound of his voice the tempest ceased at once, and the dashing waves grew quiet and calm.

The disciples were surprised to see that their master had power even greater than the power of the tempest. They were surprised to know that even the wind and the waves obeyed the voice of the Son of Man. And they asked each other, wonderingly, "What manner of person is Jesus, that even the sea obeys him?" They did not know that he had helped the great Father-God in the beginning of the creation, when the world was made.

Questions and Answers

1. Why did the disciples of Jesus become frightened one night on the Sea of Galilee? (Their boat was beginning to sink because of the fury of the storm.)

2. How did Jesus help his disciples? (With a word of command he calmed the storm, and the sea grew quiet.)

3. What did the disciples then think of Jesus? (They were surprised that he had power over the storm.)

FEEDING THE MULTITUDE

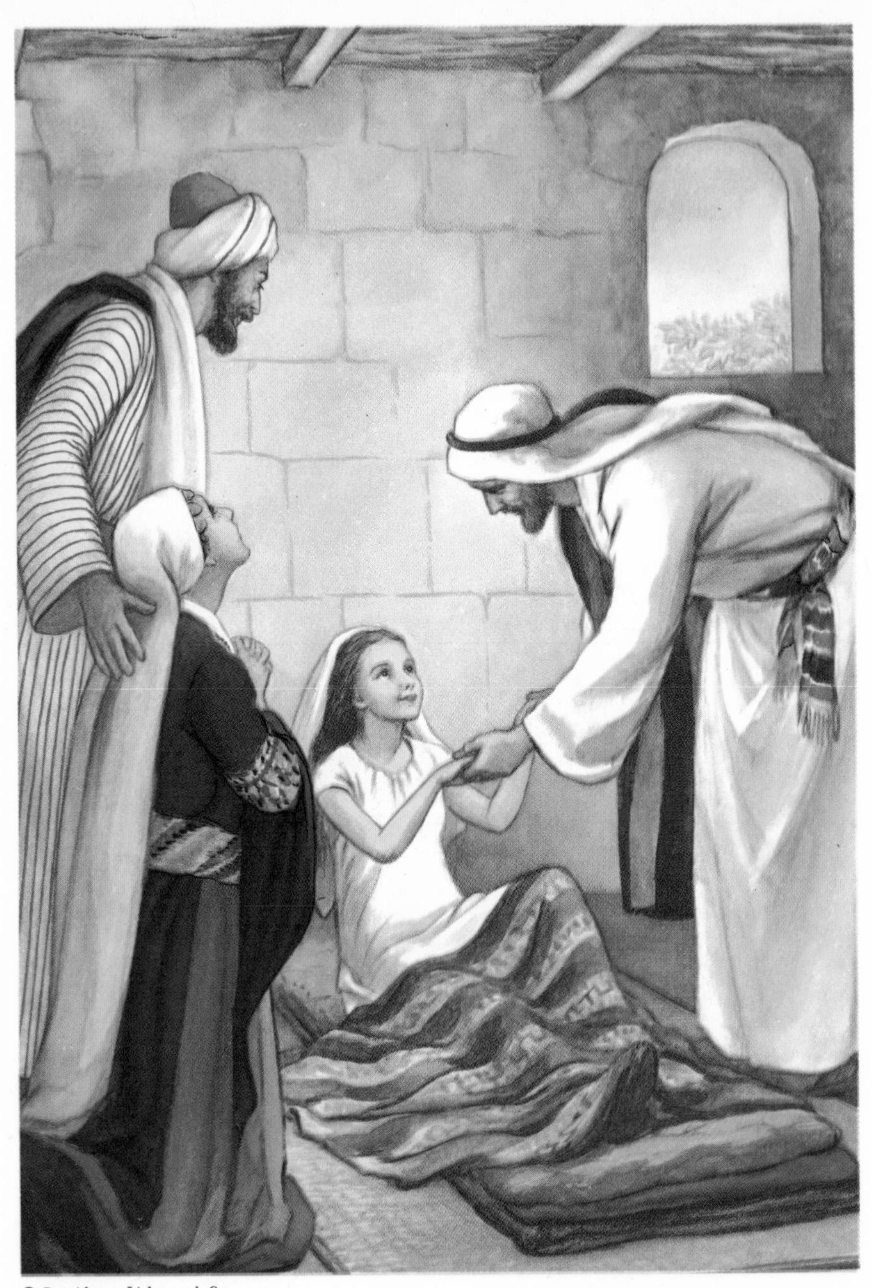

JESUS ANSWERING A CALL FOR HELP

STORY 24

Jesus Answers a Call for Help

Matt. 9:18—10:42; Mark 5:22-43; Luke 8:41—9:6

Jesus and his disciples had just returned by ship to Capernaum. There was a crowd on the shore eager to welcome them back. And again Jesus taught them and healed the sick people they brought to him.

Presently a man came running to Jesus, looking very much distressed. He fell down at Jesus' feet and cried, "My little daughter is lying at home ready to die; but if you will come with me and touch her, I know she will be made well."

This man was a ruler of the synagogue in Capernaum, and his name was Jairus. Perhaps Jesus knew this man, for often he had taught in the synagogue. Now he started at once to go with Jairus to heal his daughter. The disciples, too, went with him. And the crowd followed, eager to see another miracle. As they went, the people pressed close to Jesus, for everyone was eager to walk as near to him as possible.

In this throng was one poor woman who had been ill for twelve years. She had spent all her money in taking treatments from doctors, yet they did not cure her. Now she had no more money and still she was greatly afflicted. But she had heard of Jesus' power to heal, and this glad news brought courage to her sad heart. She decided to go to him and be made well.

How hard it was to reach him! But this woman pressed her way through the crowd till she came very near. She thought in her heart, "I will not ask him to make me well; I will only touch the hem of his garment and I know I shall be healed." So she edged her way closer, until she could reach out her hand and touch Jesus' clothes. Immediately she felt the healing power and she stepped backward into the crowd.

But Jesus knew what the woman had done. He knew about her earnest desire to be made well. So he turned around and asked, "Who touched me?"

The disciples were amazed at this question. "Why do you ask who touched you, when the people are pressing against you from every side?" they inquired.

But Jesus answered, "Someone has touched me, for I felt healing virtue go from my body."

Then the woman knew that her act was known by Jesus, and she came trembling and fell down before him, telling her sad story. Jesus spoke comforting words to her, and said, "Daughter, your faith has made you well; go in peace."

Jairus stood by waiting impatiently for Jesus to start again. He was fearful that his little daughter might die before they could reach her bedside. And sure enough, a servant from his house came to meet them with the sad news that the little girl was dead. "Do not trouble the Master any longer, for it is too late," he said.

Jesus heard the message, and saw the grief of Jairus. He said to the father, "Do not be afraid; only believe, and she shall yet be made well." So they journeyed on.

At the ruler's home many friends and neighbors had gathered to weep with the sorrowing mother and to comfort her. Jesus told them to cease their weeping, for the child was not dead, but sleeping. They did not understand that Jesus meant to say, "Death is only a sleep from which we shall all waken again." And they scoffed at his words; for they knew the little girl was dead.

Then Jesus sent everyone out of the room except the father and mother of the little girl and three of his disciples. Simon Peter and James and John were the three whom he permitted to remain with him. When the others had gone out, he took the child's hand in his own and said, "Little girl, rise up!" At his command she opened her eyes and rose up to walk about the room. Jesus told her parents to give her some food to eat, and he asked them to tell no one what he had done. Already the people were thronging him, and news of this miracle would draw greater crowds than ever.

When they left the home of Jairus, two blind men followed Jesus, crying out, "O son of David, have mercy on us!" They followed him into the house where he was staying, and when they came to him there he asked, "Do you believe that I am able to open your blind eyes?"

They answered quickly, "Yes, Lord." He touched their eyes and said, "Let it be done to you just as you believe." And their eyes were opened so that they could see.

Afterwards there was brought to Jesus a dumb man who had an evil spirit dwelling in him. And Jesus cast out the spirit, and caused the man to be able to speak. Many onlookers were amazed at these mighty miracles of Jesus, and they said, "It was never so seen in Israel." But the faultfinding Pharisees said, "He does not cast out evil spirits by the power of God, but by the power of Satan." They were jealous of the fame that had come to Jesus, and they spoke evil of him.

So great were the crowds that pressed to hear Jesus that he saw he could not teach them all. Then he sent his twelve disciples to preach in other cities, and he gave them power to heal the sick and to cast out evil spirits, and even to raise the dead. The work was too great for him to do alone, and he had chosen these men to help him. So they went to other towns and villages, preaching the gospel and healing the sick, just as Jesus commanded them to do.

Questions and Answers

1. Why did Jairus ask Jesus to come to his house? (He wanted Jesus to heal his little daughter, who was dying.)

2. Who in the crowd was healed when she touched the hem of Jesus' garment? (A woman who had been sick twelve years.)

3. What happened to the daughter of Jairus before Jesus reached her bedside? (She died.)

4. How did Jesus change sorrow into joy in Jairus' home? (He brought life into the body of the girl who had died.)

STORY 25

A Boy's Lunch Basket

Matt. 14:13-23; Mark 6:31-46; Luke 9:7-17; John 6:1-15

A boy's lunch basket is a very small thing compared with a great miracle. In this story we shall see how a great miracle grew out of a boy's lunch basket. It all came about in this manner:

The disciples whom Jesus sent to preach in the towns and cities of Galilee had returned joyfully, telling their Master about their success in healing the sick and in casting out the evil spirits, just as they had seen him do. And now the fame of Jesus was increasing every day, and many more people from distant parts of the country were flocking to hear him.

So urgent were the people who came to hear Jesus and to have their loved ones healed, that they pressed constantly upon him, and allowed no time for him to rest or even to eat. Then Jesus called his twelve disciples aside from the multitude and said, "Come with me to a quiet place, for we must rest a while."

Taking a ship they sailed away from the multitude to the other side of the sea, and went into a desert place near a mountain. But they did not find much time to rest, even in this lonely spot, for soon they saw a great throng of people coming toward them. The multitude had followed from the other side of the sea. Perhaps the disciples were disappointed because the people had found them again, but Jesus looked pityingly upon the great throng, and said of them, "They are like sheep that have no shepherd. They wander about here and there hunting for their own pasture grounds."

In this great throng were five thousand men, who had come from different parts of Galilee. Some of them had brought their wives and children along, and other women had come, too. When they had started they did not know they would have to go so very far to find Jesus, and many of them had brought nothing to eat. One boy, however, had not forgotten his lunch basket, and in his basket he carried five little loaves of barley bread and two small fishes.

When the multitude came near, Jesus received them kindly and sat down to teach them again. He healed the sick ones whom they had brought to him, and taught them many things about the kingdom of heaven.

After a while the day wore on and evening came. Still the people lingered near, seeming to forget they could find no food nor shelter in the desert place. The disciples grew impatient with them and came to ask Jesus to send them away. "They have brought no food," said the disciples, "and we cannot supply food for them in this wilderness; therefore send them away that they may buy food in the towns and villages as they journey home."

But Jesus answered, "We must feed them before sending them away." Turning to Philip, he asked, "Where shall we find bread, that all these people may eat?"

Philip looked at the great multitude and shook his head. "If we should buy two hundred pennyworth of bread," he answered, "there would not be enough for each one to have a small piece."

While Jesus and the disciples were discussing what to do, the boy who had not forgotten to carry his lunch came near and heard their conversation. Then he showed his basket of food to one of the disciples, and he offered to give the food to Jesus. The disciple, who was Andrew, came and told Jesus what the boy had said. "How many loaves are there in the basket?" asked Jesus.

"Only five and two small fishes," Andrew said. "But what will that be among so many people?"

"Bring them to me," Jesus replied. Then he told his disciples to bid the people sit down in groups, in some fifty and in others a hundred, and wait for their evening meal. While they waited, he took the little loaves and the fishes and blessed them and broke them into small pieces. He filled a basket for each of the twelve disciples and sent them to pass the food among the hungry people. Then the disciples returned, and again he filled their empty baskets. When all the people had eaten, he sent the disciples to gather up the scraps that had been left over, and they found twelve baskets full of scraps. And everyone in the great multitude had eaten all he wanted. The boy who had brought the lunch basket to Jesus had all that he could eat, and he shared his little lunch with everyone in the great throng because he had let Jesus bless his offering.

This unusual miracle caused much excitement among the people. They wanted Jesus to become their king instead of letting the Roman government rule them any longer. They believed that he could set them free from the rule of the Romans, whom they hated. They thought it would be wonderful to have a king rule them who could feed them by working miracles.

But Jesus would not allow the people to take him for their king. Although he was a King, yet he had not come to earth to rule an earthly kingdom. He commanded his disciples to enter their ship at once and return to the other side of the sea. And when they left him, he dismissed the multitude and went alone upon the mountain near by to pray.

Questions and Answers

1. Why did the people follow Jesus into the desert place? (Some came to hear his teaching; others, to be healed.)

2. Why did Jesus feel sorry for them? (They had listened to him all day and now were tired and hungry.)

3. How many had brought lunch with them? (One boy, who had five loaves of bread and two fishes.)

4. Who found him and brought him to Jesus? (Andrew.)

5. How did Jesus feed the people? (He blessed the boy's lunch, and it increased until there was enough food to satisfy the hungry multitude.)

STORY 26

The Man Who Walked on the Water

Matt. 14:23-36; Mark 6:46-56; John 6:16-29

While Jesus was alone praying on the mountainside, the disciples were in their ship rowing toward Capernaum. And the multitude were returning homeward as they had come, walking along the northern shore of the sea.

After nightfall a strong wind began to blow across the sea, driving against the little ship. Row as hard as they might, the disciples could not make much progress against the wind. Higher and higher the waves dashed and rolled, and slower the vessel plowed through them. How tired the disciples were growing! Perhaps they were thinking about the time when a tempest swept over the sea and Jesus had been with them, sleeping in the ship. Perhaps they were wishing for his presence now, to still this stormy wind that made their progress so wearisome and so slow.

Far away on the mountain Jesus had been praying for several hours. But he had not forgotten his disciples. Perhaps he had been praying for them as well as for himself. He knew how much they needed him when the

PETER COMING TO JESUS ON THE WATER

strong wind began to blow against their little ship, and he started to go to them. Out across the water he walked as easily as if it had been land, and nearer and nearer he came to the tossing ship and its weary sailors. By and by he came very near, so near that they could see him through the darkness, walking past them on the rough waves.

Now the disciples were frightened; for every one had seen Jesus, and they believed they had seen a spirit. They did not think he could really walk on water, for no person had ever done that. And they cried out for fear of what they had seen.

Jesus stopped when he heard their cry, and turned to speak to them. He said, "Do not be afraid, for it is I."

How familiar that voice sounded! Still the disciples could scarcely believe it was Jesus who spoke. Simon Peter cried out, "Lord, if it is you, bid me come to you walking on the water."

Jesus answered, "Come."

With a bound Simon Peter leaped over the side of the ship and started to go to Jesus. The other disciples looked on in amazement, wondering more than ever at the great power of Jesus. Presently, however, they saw their fellow disciple beginning to sink in the rough waves, and they heard his voice calling frantically to Jesus to help. For Simon Peter had begun to look about at the stormy wind and waves, and just as soon as he took his eyes off Jesus he began to sink. Then Jesus reached forth his hand and caught him, saying, "O man of little faith, why did you doubt?"

When the two came to the ship, the other disciples received them joyfully, and at once the wind ceased. Again the disciples marveled at the wonderful power of their master, who could perform miracles on the sea as well as on the land. And they came to him, worshiping him and saying, "Surely you are the Son of God."

Questions and Answers

1. Where was Jesus when the disciples were rowing against the wind-blown waves? (He was praying on the mountainside.)
2. How did Jesus come to them across the water? (Walking on the waves.)
3. Why were the disciples frightened when they saw Jesus? (They supposed he was a spirit.)
4. Why did Simon Peter begin to sink into the sea? (He looked at the waves instead of looking straight to Jesus.)
5. What happened after Jesus brought Peter safely into the ship? (The wind stopped blowing at once.)

STORY 27

What a Multitude Learned about Jesus

Matt. 15:29-39; Mark 7:31—8:10

Leaving Phoenicia, Jesus and his twelve disciples journeyed around to the country on the eastern side of the Sea of Galilee. A multitude of eager people gathered to see and to hear him. They followed him to a dreary country place and for three days listened to his teachings. They brought their sick people to him. And Jesus healed every one who was brought to him.

Among that number was a man who could neither hear nor speak plainly. Friends brought him to Jesus, and Jesus took him aside from the multitude, put his fingers into the man's ears, touched his tongue, then looked up to heaven and sighed, and said, "Be opened!" And immediately the man's ears were unstopped so that he was no longer deaf, and his tongue was loosed so that he could speak plainly. When the multitude saw what Jesus had done, they were astonished. And they said of him, "He has done all things well: he makes both the deaf to hear and the dumb to speak."

On the evening of the third day Jesus called his disciples aside and reminded them of how long the people

HEALING BY THE SEA OF GALILEE

had been with them without food. He said, "I am sorry for them because they have nothing to eat. We cannot send them away to their homes in this condition, for they are weak and may faint by the way."

"How can we feed them all in this desert place?" asked the disciples.

Jesus answered, "How many loaves do you have?"

They said, "Only seven, and a few little fishes."

Jesus then turned to the multitude and commanded them to sit down. When they had obeyed he took the loaves and fishes and blessed them, just as he had done when he fed the five thousand from the boy's lunch basket. The loaves and the fishes increased until there was food enough for everyone. More than four thousand people were fed by this miracle, and seven baskets of food remained after all had eaten their fill.

Then Jesus dismissed the multitude, and they returned to their homes with their sick ones made well. How glad they were that Jesus had come to visit their country!

Questions and Answers

1. How long did the crowds stay with Jesus in the desert without food? (Three days.)

2. Why did Jesus tell his disciples to feed the people before sending them away? (He knew they might faint from weakness.)

3. How many loaves did Jesus have with which to feed this throng? (Seven loaves and a few little fishes.)

4. How many people were fed? (More than four thousand.)

STORY 28

How Peter Answered a Question

Matt. 16:13-28; Mark 8:27—9:1; Luke 9:18-27

One day, while Jesus and his disciples journeyed north, to a city called Caesarea Philippi, not far from Mount Hermon, Jesus asked the disciples some questions. First he asked, "Who do men say that I am?"

The disciples answered, "Some say you are Elijah, the prophet, come back to earth; some think you are John the Baptist risen from the dead; others believe you are Jeremiah, the old prophet, or another of the old prophets who used to teach their fathers long ago."

Then Jesus asked, "But who do you men believe that I am?"

Simon Peter answered boldly, "We believe that you are Christ, the promised Messiah and King, and the Son of the living God."

Jesus told Simon Peter that God the Father had caused him to believe this, for of a truth he was the Son of the living God. But he asked the disciples to tell no one that he was the Christ, for the time had not yet come for this truth to be known publicly.

From this time Jesus began to talk to the disciples about the sorrows that would come upon them at Jerusalem when he should be taken from them and put to death by enemies among their own people. The disciples could not understand these words, for they believed Jesus would soon be their king and that they should rise to prominent places in his kingdom. They were displeased to hear him speak about dying and about rising on the third day.

Simon Peter, who often spoke for all the Twelve, took Jesus aside and said, "These terrible things will never happen to you!"

But Jesus looked sadly upon his disciples and answered, "You speak as Satan, the tempter; for your words are pleasing to man but not pleasing to God."

How much easier it would have been for Jesus to accept a throne and an earthly kingdom than to suffer and to die! Never would he yield to Satan's wishes, though he must suffer the greatest agony. But Peter and the other disciples could not understand.

Afterwards Jesus called other people to him, and when they had come he began to teach them what it would mean to be one of his followers. He said, "If anyone follows me, he must not try to please himself. He must be willing to bear his cross. And he must not try to save his own life; for he who saves his life shall lose it, but he who loses his life for my sake shall find it. And what is a man profited even if he should gain the whole world and lose his own soul? And what will a man give in exchange for his soul?"

These questions caused the people to wonder at his teachings. Then Jesus said, "The Son of Man shall come in the glory of his Father, with his angels; and then he shall reward every man according to his works."

Questions and Answers

1. What great question did Jesus ask his disciples one day? ("Who do you men believe I am?")

2. How did Simon Peter answer that question? (He said, "We believe you are Christ, the Son of the living God.")

3. Why were the disciples displeased when Jesus talked about dying and rising on the third day? (They expected Jesus to set up an earthly kingdom in which they would have prominent places.)

STORY 29

Strange Happenings on a Mountainside

Matt. 17:1-13; Mark 9:2-13; Luke 9:28-36

It had been a long, hard climb up the rough slope of the great mountain near Caesarea Philippi, and Simon Peter, James, and John were very tired when at last they found a resting place far above the quiet valley. These fishermen had not been accustomed to mountain climbing, and perhaps they would have chosen to row a boat all day rather than to take such a weary journey. But Jesus, their master, had asked them to go with him to a place of prayer, and because they loved him they had followed.

Now that they had come with him all the way up the mountain, they felt too tired to pray, and so they fell asleep, leaving Jesus to pray alone.

While the three disciples were sleeping, a great change came over their master. His face began to shine as the brightness of the sun; his clothing, too, gleamed as white as snow. Two men from heaven came to talk with him. They were Moses, the man who had spent forty days alone with God on Mount Sinai when he was leading the Israelites from Egypt to Canaan; and Elijah, the prophet who had heard God's voice on Mount Horeb, where he had gone to escape the wrath of a wicked queen. Moses had written the law of God which the Jews had as a part of their Bible, and Elijah was one of the prophets through whom God had spoken to his people in other days.

While these two heavenly visitors were talking with Jesus, the disciples awoke from their sleep. How surprised they were to see their master clothed in such brightness and talking with Moses and Elijah! They gazed in astonishment upon the glorious scene before them. Then as Moses and Elijah began to disappear from their sight Simon Peter exclaimed, "Lord, it is good for us to be here! If you are willing, let us build three tabernacles—one for you, one for Moses, and one for Elijah."

But while Peter spoke, a bright cloud descended upon the disciples, and they felt afraid. Then a voice spoke from the bright cloud and said, "This is my beloved Son, in whom I am well pleased; hear him." When the disciples heard the voice they fell to the ground, trembling with fright.

After the voice spoke, the cloud lifted, and Jesus came and touched the disciples, saying, "Rise up, and do not be afraid." When they lifted their eyes they saw Jesus only; for the bright cloud had vanished, and the heavenly visitors, too, had disappeared. Now they believed that surely Jesus is the Son of God.

On the next day, when they came down from the mountain, Jesus told them to keep this wonderful event secret among themselves until after he should rise from the dead. The disciples wondered why he should be talking about pain and grief and death when he, the Son of God, had been visited with such heavenly glory. But they were careful to tell no one about what had happened when they were alone with Jesus on the mountain.

Now the disciples asked, "Why do our teachers say that Elijah must first come before the Messiah appears?"

Jesus answered, "Elijah has come already, but they have not known him, and they have treated him shamefully. So also will they treat me."

And the disciples knew that he was speaking of John the Baptist, whom Herod had caused to be killed in prison.

Questions and Answers

1. Which of the twelve disciples did Jesus take with him up on the mountain? (Simon Peter, James, and John.)
2. What did these disciples do while Jesus prayed? (They slept.)
3. What wonderful persons did they see when they awoke? (Jesus, shining as the sun, talking with two heavenly visitors, Moses and Elijah.)
4. What did Simon Peter wish to do? (He wanted to build tabernacles for Jesus and his visitors.)
5. What did the voice from heaven say? ("This is my beloved Son; hear him.")

JESUS HELPING AN ANXIOUS FATHER

STORY 30

Jesus Helps an Anxious Father

Matt. 17:14-21; Mark 9:14-29; Luke 9:37-45

The next day after Jesus had appeared in glory on the mountain, he came with his three disciples back to the valley where he had left the nine. And he found them surrounded by a questioning throng.

As soon as Jesus came near, a man ran from the throng and fell at his feet, crying, "Lord, have mercy on my son; for he is a lunatic, and often he falls into the fire, or into the water. And I brought him to your disciples, but they could not cure him."

Jesus was grieved because he saw how little faith men had in him. He said to the troubled father, "Bring your child to me." So the man hurried to bring the boy.

When they came, the evil spirit seized the boy again and threw him violently upon the ground. There he lay in the dust, wallowing and foaming, and all the people were gazing in astonishment upon him. Jesus asked the father, "How long has your son been so afflicted?"

And the father answered, "Ever since he was a small child. Often the evil spirit has tried to destroy him; but if you can do anything for us, have mercy upon us and help us!"

Jesus saw that this man lacked faith in his power to

heal this son. He answered, "If you can believe, all things are possible to him who believes."

Then the father cried out, weeping, "O Lord, I do believe; help me to be rid of all doubt."

Jesus commanded the evil spirit to come out of the boy and torment him no longer. Then the spirit gave a loud cry and, tearing the child, came out, leaving him to lie still and unconscious upon the ground. The people rushed up to the place and said, "He is dead."

Jesus stooped down, took his limp hand, and lifted him up. The boy rose, and Jesus brought him to his father. a well child.

Then Jesus took his disciples away from the people, and they entered into a house alone. Here the nine asked their master, "Why was it that we could not cast out that evil spirit?"

Jesus answered, "Because you did not have faith. However, this kind goes out only when you fast and pray." Then Jesus talked to his disciples about their need of having faith in God.

Questions and Answers

1. How had the nine disciples failed when Jesus was not with them? (They could not heal a boy who was brought to them.)

2. Who came running to meet Jesus when he came down from the mountain with the three disciples? (The father of the boy.)

3. Why had the nine failed to heal the boy? (They did not have faith.)

4. Tell how Jesus made him well. (He commanded the evil spirit to come out of the boy, and it obeyed.)

THE SERVANT BEGGING FORGIVENESS

THE SERMON ON THE MOUNT

STORY 31

Jesus and His Disciples in Capernaum

Matt. 18:1-14; Mark 9:30-43; Luke 9:43-50

Leaving the north country near Caesarea Philippi, Jesus and his twelve disciples journeyed back to Capernaum. As they went, Jesus talked with them again about the sufferings that would soon come upon him. He even told them that he should be killed and that on the third day he would rise again. But they could not understand.

Soon the disciples fell to disputing among themselves which should be the greatest in the kingdom of heaven. They still believed that Jesus would set up an earthly kingdom and that they should hold positions of honor in that kingdom. But as they disputed among themselves they said nothing to Jesus about the matter, not until after they had reached Capernaum.

When all the disciples were come together in the house, Jesus asked them what they had been disputing about on the way to Capernaum. They were ashamed to tell; but Jesus knew their thoughts and he knew, too, what they had said to one another as they walked along the dusty road leading from Caesarea Philippi. So he called a little child to him. Taking the child in his arms, he said, "No one shall even be able to enter the kingdom of heaven unless he becomes like a little child. And whoever humbles himself as this little child is willing to do shall be the greatest in the kingdom of heaven."

Jesus then told the disciples to be careful not to despise little children. And he warned them to be careful lest they cause some child to lose faith in him. "For," he said, "it is not the will of your Father who is in heaven that one of these little children should lose faith in me and die in sin."

One of the disciples, named John, then spoke to Jesus and told him that they had seen a man casting out evil spirits in Jesus' name, and he was not a follower with them. "We forbade him to cast out evil spirits any more in your name, because he would not follow with us," said John.

Jesus replied, "You should not have done so; for whoever performs a miracle in my name is helping me in my great work, although he does not walk with us."

Questions and Answers

1. What lesson did Jesus try to teach his disciples with a little child? (A lesson in humility.)

2. Who did Jesus say would be greatest in the kingdom of heaven? (Those persons who would humble themselves and become like little children.)

3. What did Jesus teach his disciples about little children? (The heavenly Father wills that children keep their faith in Jesus.)

"HOW OFTEN SHALL I FORGIVE?"

STORY 32

Jesus Teaches Peter a Lesson

Matt. 18:21-35

One day Simon Peter came to Jesus and asked, "Lord, how often shall I forgive my brother if he sins against me and then asks my pardon? Shall I forgive him seven times?"

Perhaps Peter did not have much patience with a man who would sin against him often and always ask to be forgiven. Perhaps he thought no person could be truly sorry for his wrongdoing if he should have to ask so many times to be forgiven.

Jesus replied, "I do not say that you shall forgive him seven times only, but seventy times seven."

How surprised Peter must have been when he heard this answer! He may have wondered whether he could ever truly forgive a man so many times as that.

Jesus told Peter a story about a king whose servant owed him a great amount of money. The king called this servant and asked him to pay the debt. But the servant had nothing with which to pay, for he had spent all the money. Then the king said, "Because you cannot pay me the money you borrowed, I will command that you and your wife and your children be sold, and that all of your property be taken away from you. In this way I can regain some of the money you borrowed and have lost."

The servant felt very sad when he heard these words, and he fell on his face before the king, crying, "O King, have patience with me and I will pay every penny I owe!"

Because the king had a kind heart he felt sorry for the man. He told him to rise up and go away to his own house. He said, "I will forgive all the debt, and you need not try to pay it back."

After this servant went out from the king's presence he met a very poor man who had borrowed only a few dollars from him. He asked the man to pay it back, but the man could not. Then the servant became very angry, and seizing the poor man by the throat, he cried, "Pay back what you borrowed or I will throw you into the prison house and keep you there until you do!"

Then the poor man fell down at his feet and cried out, "Have patience with me, and I will pay every penny I owe."

The king's servant would not listen and, because the poor man had no money, he threw him into the prison.

Other servants of the king were standing by and they saw how unkindly this poor man had been treated. They knew how the king had just forgiven the unkind man a very great debt, and they felt sad because he had been unwilling to forgive the small debt of his poor neighbor. They went to the king and told him how unmercifully the servant had treated his poor neighbor after having been forgiven this great debt.

The king was surprised to hear that his servant whom he had treated so kindly should dare to be so unkind to another. He quickly sent for him. The king was angry, and when the unkind servant came in he said, "O wicked man, I forgave all your debt because you could not pay, and should you not have been willing to forgive the small debt your poor neighbor owed? Because you have dared to be so wicked after I had pity on you, now I will cast you into the prison house until you pay all you owed me in the first place."

When Jesus finished the story he said to Peter, "If you refuse from your heart to forgive the wrongdoings of those who sin against you, neither will my heavenly Father forgive your great sins against him."

Questions and Answers

1. What question did Peter ask Jesus about forgiveness? (He asked whether seven times were often enough to forgive his brother.)
2. How many times did Jesus say Peter should forgive his brother? (Seventy times seven times.)
3. How may God be likened to the king in the story which Jesus told Peter? (When God forgives the repentant sinner, he expects that man to forgive those who have wronged him.)
4. Why is it necessary that we forgive others? (God will not forgive anyone who is unwilling to forgive others.)

STORY 33

The Unfriendly Samaritans

Luke 9:51-56

One day Jesus and his twelve disciples left Capernaum and took the south road leading through the country of Samaria. They were going to Jerusalem. On their way they came to a certain village in Samaria where Jesus wished to spend the night, and he sent messengers to find a place for him and for his disciples to rest.

But the Samaritans in the village would not permit Jesus and his disciples to stop with them. They would not allow them to rest in their village. They knew Jesus and his disciples were Jews, and the Jews had often been unkind to their people. Now they, too, would be unkind.

Two of the disciples, James and his brother John, were very much annoyed by the unfriendly actions of these village people. They felt that their master had been mistreated, and they wished to see the villagers punished. They remembered how Elijah, the prophet, had once called fire down from heaven to destroy some wicked people, and now they came to Jesus and asked, "Will you permit us to call fire down from heaven to destroy these unkind people who have turned us away?"

Jesus answered, "Your desire is not good, for the Son

of Man is not come to destroy men's lives, but to save them."

Then he went with his disciples to another village.

Questions and Answers

1. Why did two of Jesus' disciples wish to call fire from heaven to destroy a Samaritan village? (The Samaritans refused them lodging for the night.)

2. What reply did Jesus give when they asked his permission to do this? (He said, "The Son of man is not come to destroy men's lives, but to save them.")

3. What did Jesus and his disciples do after the Samaritans refused to permit them to stop in their village? (They went to another village.)

JOURNEYING THROUGH SAMARIA

THE LEPERS ASKING JESUS FOR HELP

STORY 34

The Ten Lepers

Luke 9: 57-62; 17: 11-19

As Jesus and his disciples journeyed a man came to Jesus and said, "Lord, I too would follow you wherever you go." No doubt he believed, as did the disciples, that Jesus would soon be the great king of the Jews for whom so many were looking, and he desired to be a friend of such a great person.

Jesus answered, "Foxes have holes in the ground for their homes, and birds of the air have nests; but the Son of Man is so poor that he has not even a place of his own to lay his head."

Ten men who were lepers saw Jesus and his disciples passing by. These men had heard about how Jesus had healed other lepers, and now they called loudly to him, for they stood far off, "Jesus, Master, have mercy on us!"

Never did Jesus pass by and refuse to help one who called earnestly to him. He stopped and called back to the lepers, telling them to go and show themselves to the priests, as Moses had commanded every leper to do who was healed. They understood what Jesus meant, and they started at once to go to the priests for an examination. And as they went the leprosy left their bodies and they were made every bit well.

One of these lepers stopped and turned back just as soon as he saw that his leprosy had gone from him. He ran to Jesus and fell down before him, worshiping him and thanking him for the miracle he had performed. And this man was not a Jew, but a Samaritan. The other men, however, hurried on their way, never stopping to thank the great healer.

And Jesus said to the disciples, "Were there not ten lepers who were made well? But where are the nine? There is none turned back to give thanks except this stranger who is a Samaritan."

Then he said to the man kneeling at his feet, "Rise up and go your way, for your faith has made you well."

Questions and Answers

1. What did the ten lepers ask of Jesus? (They asked him to heal them.)
2. What happened as they hurried to obey Jesus? (They were healed.)
3. How many returned first to thank Jesus for what he had done? (Only one.)
4. To what people did the thankful man belong? (He was a Samaritan.)

JESUS SPEAKING IN THE TEMPLE

STORY 35

Jesus at a Great Feast in Jerusalem

John 7:2-53

Summer had passed, and the cooler days of autumn had come again. On the green hillsides around Jerusalem many booths, or huts, made of the branches of trees, stood in groups, sheltering the people who had come to attend the Feast of Tabernacles, held every year in this city. And during the week of the Feast the Temple was crowded with visitors from other parts of the land.

On the first day after the Feast began, groups of people stood together talking about the great Teacher in Galilee, whose miracles had caused much excitement in many places. They wondered whether he would come to Jerusalem and teach them there. Some of them wished he would come, for they enjoyed hearing him teach; others wished he would come because they hated him and wanted to find occasion to put him to death.

By and by Jesus came, and straight into the Temple he went, to sit down there and teach the people. His enemies believed this would be a good opportunity to catch him, so they sent men to listen to his words and to find some fault, that they might accuse him to the rulers.

Day after day passed by and still Jesus sat in the

Temple, teaching all who came to him. No one attempted to drive him away, and no one took hold of him to capture him. Many of the Jews who lived in Jerusalem knew how much their leaders hated him, and they wondered why these men did not take him now and shut him up in prison. They said, "Is this not he whom they seek to kill? But now he speaks boldly and they say nothing to him. Have they come to believe that he is the very Christ?"

But the rulers of the Jews—who were the chief priests in the Temple, and the scribes, and the Pharisees, and the Sadducees—did not acknowledge that Jesus is the Christ. They were very jealous of him because he drew the attention of all the people who came to the Feast. They disliked his teaching because he accused them of only pretending to be righteous. And they sent officers to take him.

Even the officers were pleased to hear the teaching of this wonderful man from Galilee. They listened carefully to his words, and they believed that he was not worthy to be punished. So they returned to the rulers without him.

The chief priests and Pharisees were angry when the officers returned alone. They asked, "Why have you not brought him?"

The officers replied, "Never did a man speak like this man." And they would not harm him.

The men who sent the officers were excited. They

asked, "Are you allowing this man to deceive you as he is deceiving the other people? And have any of our own number of the rulers believed on him?"

Nicodemus, the Pharisee who had come to visit Jesus one night, sat among the angry rulers. He loved Jesus and believed in him. But he was afraid to let the other Pharisees know, for fear they would hate him too. Now he asked timidly, "Does our law judge any man before it hears him and knows what he is doing?"

His angry friends turned on him and replied, scornfully, "Are you from Galilee? Do you not know that no prophet comes from that country?" And they dismissed their meeting and went to their homes.

Questions and Answers

1. What great feast was held each autumn in Jerusalem? (The Feast of Tabernacles.)
2. What did Jesus do at the Feast? (Taught the people in the Temple.)
3. Why did the officers whom his enemies had sent refuse to capture Jesus? (They said of him, "Never did a man speak like this man.")
4. How was Nicodemus unlike the other Pharisees? (He believed in Jesus.)

JESUS WITH THE PHARISEES

STORY 36

Jesus Answers a Question

John 8

Early the next morning after the officers had failed to take Jesus, the scribes and Pharisees had planned another way to capture him. They would go themselves and ask him a great question concerning the teaching of the law of Moses. Already they thought they knew how he would answer, and then they would have opportunity to find fault with him.

Jesus was in the Temple when his enemies came, bringing with them a very wicked woman whom the law of Moses commanded should be punished by death. They went straight to Jesus and said, "Master, this woman is very wicked, and Moses in the law has commanded that such a person should be stoned until she dies. But what do you say we should do to her?"

Jesus knew they were tempting him, and at first he paid no attention to them. He stooped down and with his finger wrote in the dust of the ground. But those enemies would not be gotten rid of so easily. Now they believed they had caught him in a trap, and they kept asking until finally he raised up, and looked at them and said, "Let the man among you who is without sin cast the first stone at her." Then he stooped down again and continued to write with his finger in the dust.

The men were much surprised at his reply to their question. They looked at each other, then at the woman who stood trembling, and their own consciences reminded them of their sins. The older men shook their heads and turned to go away. The younger men, too, felt the accusations of their own guilty consciences, and they followed the older men out of the Temple.

When all the men had gone out, Jesus looked up from the ground and saw only the woman standing before him. He asked, "Woman, where are those men who accused you of this great sin? Did no one condemn you?"

She replied, "No man, Lord."

Then he said, "Neither do I condemn you; go, and do not commit sin any more." So she, too, turned and went away.

Many people were now gathering in the Temple, and Jesus began to teach them again. He began by saying, "I am the light of the world: the man who follows me shall not walk in darkness, but shall have the light of life."

The Pharisees who heard him began to accuse him, saying, "Your words are not true, because you speak of your own self."

Jesus answered that even though he did speak of himself, he knew that his words were true, for he knew who had sent him into the world and where he would go when he should leave the world. He said, "You cannot tell these things." Then he told them that another besides himself spoke of him in the same way, and that one was his Father. "Where is your Father?" they asked.

Jesus answered, "If you knew me, you would know my Father; but you know neither me nor my Father."

All that day Jesus taught in the Temple, speaking very plainly to the Jews and telling them about their sins. And the displeasure of his enemies increased more and more, until they thought they would listen no longer. For Jesus had said that if anyone would obey his words that one should never see death. Jesus meant that those who obey him would never die in sin.

His enemies did not understand, and they said, "Now we know you have an evil spirit, for Abraham is dead, and all the prophets are dead; and you say that any man who keeps your words will never die. Are you greater than our father Abraham, who is dead? And the prophets, too, are dead. Who do you claim to be?"

Jesus replied, "I do not honor myself; but my Father, whom you call your God, he it is who honors me. You have not known my Father; but I know him. If I should say I know him not, I should be speaking a lie. I know him, and I obey his words. Your father Abraham was glad when he saw my day, but you do not behave like the children of Abraham."

Now the Jews cried out, "How could you have seen our father Abraham, for you are not yet fifty years old?"

Jesus answered, "Before Abraham was, I am."

"I AM" was the name by which God was known, and the Jews were struck with horror when they heard Jesus call himself by that sacred name. They picked up stones to hurl at him, but Jesus hid himself among the people, then quietly passed out of the Temple and walked away.

Questions and Answers

1. Whom did Jesus' enemies bring to him for condemnation one day? (A woman who was a great sinner.)
2. Why did Jesus stoop down and write in the dust with his finger? (He knew they were setting a trap for him.)
3. What did Jesus finally tell them to do? (He said, "Let the man among you who is without sin cast the first stone at her.")
4. Why were the men afraid to pick up stones and throw them at the woman? (They knew in their hearts that they, too, were sinners.)
5. What did Jesus tell the woman to do? ("Go, and sin no more.")

JESUS IN THE HOME OF A PHARISEE

STORY 37

What Happened to a Blind Man

John 9

As Jesus went away from the Temple, where the angry Jews were getting ready to stone him, he saw a blind man sitting by the roadside begging. This man had always been blind, for he had been born without sight. His parents lived in Jerusalem.

The twelve disciples were with Jesus when he passed the place where the poor man sat. They knew he had been blind from his birth, and they asked Jesus whether this blindness had come upon him as a punishment for his own sin or whether it had come because of the sins of his parents. Jesus answered, "Neither this man's sins nor the sin of his parents has caused him to be without sight, but he was born blind that the works of God might be shown through him."

Then Jesus stopped. Having made a little clay he rubbed it on the blind man's eyes. Then he said to the poor man, "Go to the pool called Siloam and wash."

The blind man did not ask, "Why must I do this?" He rose at once and groped his way to the pool. Here he washed the mud off his sightless eyes, and immediately he began to see.

JESUS TOUCHING THE BLIND MAN'S EYES

Instead of returning to the roadside to beg, the happy man went home to his people, telling the good news. His neighbors and friends and even his parents were greatly surprised, because they had never expected such a miracle to happen to him. Many who saw him could hardly believe he was the same man as the blind beggar whom they had known before. They said, "He is like the beggar." But the man answered, "I am the same person."

The excitement in that neighborhood increased when the people heard that Jesus had opened the blind man's eyes. They gathered round to ask, "What did Jesus do to you? How did he open your eyes?"

The man told them that Jesus first made clay, then rubbed it on his eyes, and afterward sent him to wash in the pool of Siloam. "And I went and washed, and I received my sight," he said, joyfully, for he was a very happy man.

"Where is this Jesus now?" they asked. The man did not know where Jesus and his disciples had gone.

The neighbors brought the man who had been blind to the Pharisees, and they also questioned him. Because it was the Sabbath Day they thought Jesus had done wrong by anointing the man's eyes and sending him to wash in the pool. They said, "Give God the glory, for we know this man Jesus is a sinner." Others standing by said, "How can a man who is a sinner do such miracles?" And the people were divided, some thinking Jesus was a great man and others thinking he was only deceiving those who believed in him.

The Pharisees then asked the man what he thought of Jesus, and the man replied, "I believe he is a prophet."

The enemies of Jesus were greatly stirred by this miracle. They thought perhaps the man was only pretending, after all, that he had been born blind. So they called his parents and questioned them concerning their son.

The parents were afraid of these Jews. They knew of the hatred these men felt toward Jesus, and they knew the chief priests had threatened to cast them out of the synagogue if they believed in him. So they said, "This man is our son, and we know he was born blind. But we do not know how his eyes received sight; he is a grown man and he can tell you for himself."

Again the excited enemies of Jesus called the man who had been blind, and asked, "What did Jesus do to you? How did he open your eyes?"

The man answered, "I have told you once and you would not listen. If I tell you again will you also be his disciples?"

At this they scorned him, and said, "We are Moses' disciples, for we know that God spoke to Moses, but as for this fellow we do not know where he came from."

Now the man whom Jesus had healed grew very bold, and he said, "It is strange that you do not know where Jesus came from since he opened my eyes, which were always blind! We all know that God does not hear sinners, but if any man worships him and does his will, God hears that man. Since the world began it was never heard that any man opened the eyes of one who was born blind. If Jesus was not of God, he could do nothing."

These words stirred up more anger in the hearts of Jesus' enemies, and they said to the man, "You were born a sinner, and do you try to teach us?"

They cast him out of the synagogue, and he could no longer worship there with his people.

Jesus soon heard what the angry priests had done, and he looked about to find the man whom they had cast out of the synagogue. When he found him he asked. "Do you believe on the Son of God?"

The man answered, "Who is he, Lord, that I may believe?"

And Jesus said, "You have seen him with your eyes, and even now he is speaking to you."

Then the man rejoiced and said, "Lord, I believe!" And he worshiped Jesus there.

Questions and Answers

1. How long had the blind beggar been without his sight? (All his life.)
2. Why did Jesus send him to the pool of Siloam? (To test his faith.)
3. Who brought the man to the Pharisees? (The neighbors.)
4. Why did the Pharisees call the parents of the man who had been blind? (They thought the man might only be pretending to have been born blind.)
5. What did they do with the man when he spoke in defense of Jesus? (They cast him out of the synagogue.)

JESUS TAKING LITTLE CHILDREN IN HIS ARMS

STORY 38

Little Children Are Brought to Jesus

Matt. 19:13-15; Mark 10:13-16

While Jesus was teaching the people in a country place not far from the Jordan River, some mothers brought their little children to him and asked him to bless them.

Jesus loves children, so he took them in his arms and put his hands upon their heads and prayed.

But the disciples stood by looking much displeased. They called the mothers aside and said, "You should not trouble our master in this way, for he has more important work to do than to caress your children!"

No doubt the mothers were grieved to hear them speak these words.

Jesus, too, was grieved with the disciples.

He said, "Do not forbid the little children to come to me, for of such is the kingdom of God. Whoever of you will not receive the kingdom of God just as a little child, can never enter into it." And again he took the little ones in his loving arms to caress and to bless them.

Jesus knew that children would gladly believe him and that many times they could lead older people to believe in him too. He knew their hearts were tender and quick to respond to his love, while older people were more ready to doubt and to question whether or not he was the very Christ.

Questions and Answers

1. Why were the disciples displeased with some women one day? (Because they brought their little children to Jesus.)

2. How do we know that Jesus loves children? (He took them in his arms and blessed them.)

STORY 39

A Young Man Goes Away Sad

Matt. 19:16-30; Mark 10:14-31

As Jesus and his disciples went to another place, a young man came running to meet them. This young man was very rich, and he wore beautiful clothing. But he knelt down in the dust before Jesus, and said, "Good Master, what good thing shall I do that I may receive life in the other world?"

"Why do you call me good?" asked Jesus, adding, "for there is none good but God. You know the commandments—'Do not kill'; 'Do not steal'; 'Do not speak falsely'; 'Honor your father and your mother.' "

"Yes, I know the commandments of Moses," answered the young man, "and I have kept them from childhood. But I seem to lack something yet. O Master, tell me what it is!"

Jesus looked tenderly into the anxious face of the young man before him, and he loved this man. He longed to help him. But he knew the one thing that hindered this man from being contented and happy. He knew the one thing that stood between this man and the hope of life in the other world. Just one thing; but unless that one thing should be taken away, the rich young man

THE YOUNG MAN GOES AWAY SAD

could never enter heaven. So he said, "You lack one thing, just one. If you would be perfectly happy, go home and sell all that you have, and give your riches to the poor people. Then you will have riches in heaven. Afterwards you may come back and be my disciple."

What a change came over the young man's face when he heard these words! He bent his head forward and walked very slowly away, for he was sad and deeply troubled. Jesus watched him go away, and Jesus, too, was sad. Then he turned to the disciples and said, "How hard it is for rich men to enter into the kingdom of God!" He knew this young man loved his riches more than he loved God, and that he was unwilling to sell his possessions and give his money to the poor. Because he loved his riches he could not be contented and happy, for his heart was not right in God's sight. Always he felt that something was lacking, that something clouded his hope of life in heaven. But he turned away from Jesus, choosing rather to be rich in this world than to be a disciple of the Lord.

Questions and Answers

1. What great question did a rich young man ask of Jesus? ("What good thing must I do that I may receive eternal life?")
2. How many of Moses' commands had the young man kept? (All of them.)
3. What did Jesus tell him to do if he wished to please God? (To sell all his goods, give his money to the poor, and follow Jesus.)
4. Why did the young man turn away from Jesus with a sad heart? (Because he loved his riches more than he loved God.)

STORY 40

Seventy Other Disciples Sent Out

Luke 10:1-24

Jesus knew that he had not much longer to preach, for the time was near when he must lay down his life for the sins of the people. He therefore chose seventy other men who had followed him and received his teachings.

He gave them power to heal the sick and to cast out evil spirits. Then he sent them out, two and two, into the country east of the Jordan River, to preach in the cities and villages where he intended to go later.

And just as the twelve disciples had gone, so these men went forth to heal the sick and to tell people that the kingdom of heaven was coming near to them.

When their errand was finished they hurried back to Jesus, telling him that even the evil spirits obeyed when they commanded them to depart.

These seventy disciples rejoiced much because they had received power to command evil spirits to obey them.

But Jesus said, "Do not rejoice in this, but rather be glad because your names are written in heaven."

Then Jesus prayed to God the Father, and afterwards

THE GOOD SAMARITAN AT THE INN

THE GOOD SAMARITAN PAYING THE KEEPER OF THE INN

he turned to his disciples and said, "Blessed are the eyes that see the things you see; for I tell you that many prophets and kings desired to see the things which you see, but they did not see them, and to hear the things which you hear, but they did not hear them."

Questions and Answers

1. Why did Jesus send out seventy other disciples? (Because he needed more helpers in his great work.)

2. For what did Jesus tell them to be glad? (That their names were written in heaven.)

STORY 41

The Good Samaritan

Luke 10:25-37

One day a lawyer came to Jesus and asked a question, wishing to tempt him. He said, "Master, what shall I do to inherit life in heaven?"

Jesus was sure this man knew the law of Moses, and instead of answering the question he asked another. He said, "What is written in the law of Moses? Do you not know its teachings?"

The lawyer replied, "Moses wrote that we should love the Lord our God with all our heart, and with all our soul, and with all our strength, and with all our mind; and that we should love our neighbors as ourselves."

Jesus said, "You have answered right. Do this, and you shall have life in heaven."

But the man was not willing to turn away yet. He asked Jesus, "Who is my neighbor?"

And Jesus told him the story about the Good Samaritan. This is the story:

"One day a man started to travel from Jerusalem to Jericho. As he went along the lonely road he met some robbers. These men stopped him, took away his money, tore off his clothing, and beat him until he was half dead. Then they ran off, leaving him to lie by the roadside.

"Presently a priest came along the road, and he saw the poor man lying there. But he did not stop to help the stranger. He did not even speak to the poor man and ask if he might send some friends to aid him, but passed by on the other side of the road.

"After the priest had gone by a Levite came by. When he saw the poor man he also took no second look. He did not offer to help him. He hurried on his way, leaving the poor man to die.

"And probably the poor man would have died if a kindhearted Samaritan had not come along the road soon afterwards. When he saw the poor man he stopped his donkey, climbed off, and bent over the stranger to speak to him. He saw that the wounded man was a Jew, and he knew the Jews were not friendly to the Samaritans, but he knew this Jew was in deep trouble. He poured oil upon the wounded places and bound them up. Then he gave the wounded man a drink to revive him, and helped him to climb into the saddle on his own donkey's back. He brought the wounded man to a sheltering place called an inn, where travelers stopped overnight. Here he took care of him until the next day, and before he started on his journey again he gave money to the keeper of the inn, and said, 'Take care of this stranger until he is well, and if more money is needed I will give it when I come again.'

"Now," asked Jesus of the lawyer, "which of the three men was a neighbor to the one who was attacked by the robbers?"

"The man who treated him kindly," answered the lawyer; and Jesus said, "Go, and do as the Samaritan did."

Questions and Answers

1. How did the lawyer try to tempt Jesus? (By questioning him.)
2. Why did Jesus tell him the story about the good Samaritan? (To answer his question, "Who is my neighbor?")
3. Who did Jesus say was a neighbor? (One who helps others, even if they are his enemies.)

DISCIPLES GOING OUT, TWO BY TWO

STORY 42

Jesus Teaches in a Pharisee's House

Luke 14:1-24

Jesus knew the plans of his enemies in Jerusalem and he did not remain long in Bethany, but took his disciples and returned again to the country near the Jordan River.

One Sabbath Day a Pharisee who lived in that part of the country asked Jesus to eat dinner at his house. And Jesus went with him. Other Pharisees and lawyers were present at the dinner, and, as usual, some people were there who had not been invited. These stood about in the dining hall while the guests were eating.

Among the onlookers was one poor man who had a disease called dropsy. He had come because he heard that Jesus would be there, and he hoped Jesus would have mercy upon him and heal him. When Jesus saw the poor man he pitied him. Turning to the Pharisees and lawyers, he asked, "Is it permitted in the law to heal on the Sabbath Day?" But the men would not answer.

Jesus healed the poor man and sent him away. Then he said to the Pharisees, "If your ox or your ass fell into a pit, not one of you would allow it to remain there until after the Sabbath had passed, but you would pull the unfortunate beast out at once."

They understood that he meant to teach them to be just as merciful toward the poor man whom he had healed of the dropsy.

Those present at the dinner expected to hear Jesus teach, and they were not disappointed. He had noticed how the guests chose the best places for themselves when they arrived, and he taught them a lesson on humility. He said, "When you are invited to a wedding, do not choose for yourself the places of most honor, lest a man come who is more honorable than you. Then you will be asked to give your place to him, and you will feel ashamed before all the guests. But if you choose rather to take the lowest place, then you may be called up higher, and you will receive honor from your friends."

Jesus turned to the Pharisee who had invited him to the house, and said, "When you prepare a feast, do not invite your friends and relatives and rich neighbors; for they will reward you in the same manner. But if you wish to receive a reward at the time when the righteous people are resurrected, then invite the poor and the crippled and the blind to your feasts; for such people cannot repay you, and God will bless you."

Then Jesus spoke a parable to them all about the kingdom of God. He said:

"A certain man prepared a great supper and invited many guests. When all was ready, he sent his servant to call the invited persons to come and eat. But every one began to make an excuse to stay away. The first man said he had bought a piece of ground and would have to go at once to see it, and he asked to be excused from the supper. Another man said he had bought two oxen and he was going to try them out for driving, so he could not come. Another said he had gotten married, and he could not come. Everywhere the servant went the invited guests begged to be excused, and the servant returned to tell his master.

"The feast was ready and waiting, and the master was greatly disappointed to hear how his invited guests had refused to come. He became angry with them, and said they should not be allowed even to taste the supper he had prepared. He sent the servant out quickly to gather in the poor people from the streets, and the servant brought in the blind and the lame. And still there was room. Then the master sent the servant to the country places near by to bring in the poor people who had not been invited. And his house was filled with hungry people who enjoyed the good things he had prepared for his unfaithful friends."

Questions and Answers

1. Whom did Jesus heal one Sabbath when he dined at a Pharisee's house? (A man suffering with dropsy.)

2. How did Jesus teach the guests a lesson on humility? (He told them to seek the lowest place when invited to a wedding.)

3. What lesson did Jesus teach the guests in his parable about the kingdom of God? (The Jews were first invited into the kingdom, but they refused to come; God now welcomes everybody.)

JESUS AND THE PHARISEES

EVERY MAN HAD AN EXCUSE

STORY 43

The Pharisees Try to Frighten Jesus

Luke 13:31-33

One day some of the Pharisees came to Jesus and pretended to be friendly. They told him that Herod, the King, was seeking to take his life just as he had caused John the Baptist to be put to death. They urged Jesus to leave the country at once, lest Herod find him and kill him. They hoped in this manner to be rid of Jesus.

But Jesus did not feel afraid of Herod. He knew that his greatest enemies were among the religious rulers of the Jews. They hated him because he taught the poor people and because he told them about their sins.

Now he said to these Pharisees: "Go to Herod and tell him that I cast out evil spirits and heal the sick today and tomorrow, and on the third day I shall be made perfect. For I must walk today and tomorrow and even the day following, for it cannot be that a prophet shall perish outside of Jerusalem."

Jesus meant that just as the Jews had killed God's prophets in other days, so they would kill him.

Questions and Answers

1. Why did the Pharisees want him to go away? (They hoped to frighten Jesus away.)
2. Was Jesus frightened? (No; he knew that the Pharisees simply wanted to get rid of him.)

SHEPHERDS WITH THEIR SHEEP IN THE WILDERNESS

STORY 44

Parables by the Way

Luke 15

Many publicans and sinners followed Jesus, to hear his words. And the Pharisees and scribes found fault, saying, "This man receives sinners and even eats with them." Jesus knew how they were complaining about him, and he spoke to the people by parables. First he told them the parable about the Lost Sheep. Because the Jews kept many sheep he knew they would understand the story.

"What man of you," he asked, "having a hundred sheep would not leave the ninety-nine in the wilderness and seek for the one that was lost? And when he finds it he will bring it back and rejoice more over that sheep than over the ninety-nine which did not wander away. So it is in heaven when a sinner repents and forsakes his sins; there is more rejoicing over him than over ninety-nine just persons who have no sin."

There were women in the crowd listening to Jesus' words. And Jesus saw them there, so he told a story which they might understand. "What woman," he asked, "having ten pieces of silver and losing one of them will not search carefully through the house until she finds the missing piece? And when she finds it she tells her neighbors and friends, and asks them to rejoice with her because she has found the piece that was lost. So also there is rejoicing in heaven when one lost sinner comes to God."

Both the men and the women were listening very carefully now, and Jesus told the parable about the unthankful son who left his father's house and went to live among strangers. This is the story:

"A certain man had two sons, and the younger son was not contented to remain at home with his father and his brother. He asked that his father divide the money which would some day be given to him and to his brother, and give to him at once the part that would be his. The father divided the money, and the younger son took his part and went away. He thought he was very rich, and he spent his money freely. He enjoyed every pleasure that he knew, and he seemed to have many friends. But after a while he spent all his money and he had nothing left. Then he grew hungry; but his friends left him and refused to help.

"In his trouble the young man offered to care for a farmer's hogs, but he could scarcely keep from starving. And no man pitied him, or gave him any decent food to eat.

"Then the young man remembered his father and the hired servants who worked in his father's house. He knew those servants were well cared for. He decided to return to his father's house and ask to be made a servant there. So he returned to his home country to beg his father's forgiveness and to ask permission to be only a servant in the old home.

"That father loved his wandering boy, and his heart was sad when the boy left him to live among strangers. Every day he longed for the boy to come back. And when at last he saw his son coming, clothed in rags, he ran out to meet him and wept for joy. The boy began to speak. He said, 'Father, I have sinned against heaven and against you—'; but he had no opportunity to tell the father how he wished to become a servant in the old home. The father commanded a servant to go quickly and bring the best clothes and dress the young man in them, and to prepare a feast of gladness, for the lost had been found."

Questions and Answers

1. What three stories did Jesus tell about lost things? (The Lost Coin, the Lost Sheep, and the Prodigal Son.)

2. What do these stories teach us? (That Jesus is seeking people lost in sin, because he loves them.)

THE UNFAITHFUL STEWARD WITH HIS MASTER

STORY 45

An Unfaithful Steward

Luke 16:1-12

In the multitude which followed Jesus were people of many different villages. Some of his listeners were poor people, some were rich; some were educated; some were not. Jesus knew about their differences, and he wished to teach them all. He knew how well everyone likes to listen to a good story, so he preached some story sermons to the multitude. One of the story sermons was about an unfaithful man who was a steward.

"A certain rich man," said Jesus, "hired a servant to take care of his goods. This servant came to live in the rich man's beautiful house and was called his steward. He was supposed to handle the master's business wisely, but he did not. And after a while the master heard that the steward was wasting his goods.

"Calling the unfaithful steward, the master told him what he had heard. And the steward hung his head in shame because he could not deny his guilt. Then the master grew angry and said, 'No longer shall you be my steward!' And he was about to dismiss the servant.

"Now, the steward had no other home in which to live, and he wondered what he should do. He thought he could not work in the fields like a poor man, and he was too proud to beg for food from door to door. So he decided to make friends with the other servants of the rich man that they might receive him into their homes to live. And he hurried to do this very thing.

"By and by the master heard what the unfaithful steward was doing, and he said, 'After all, that man is careful to look out for himself. He shows much wisdom in this one thing.' "

By this story Jesus wished to teach the people that they would not always have homes in this world, for some day they would have to leave their homes and go to live in another world. And just as the unfaithful steward had shown wisdom in preparing a home for himself for the time when he should no longer have a home in the rich man's house, so the people should begin to prepare for themselves a home in heaven by trying to please God.

Questions and Answers

1. How did the unfaithful steward show wisdom? (He showed great kindness to the other servants, hoping they would take care of him when his master dismissed him.)

STORY 46

A Poor Rich Man and a Rich Beggar

Luke 16:19-31

The Pharisees seemed to think that rich people were better than poor people. One day Jesus told them a story to show that God looks at people's hearts instead of their riches.

"There was a certain rich man who thought only of his own comfort and happiness. He wore expensive clothes, like a king's, and ate the best kind of food every day. His many servants were quick to do his bidding, and he did nothing except to live and enjoy himself.

"And there was a certain beggar man named Lazarus, who had no home nor friends. He was a good man although he was a beggar, and he came to sit at the gate of the rich man to ask for crumbs which might fall from the rich man's table. The poor beggar was sick, and sores broke out all over his body. He could not drag himself away from the rich man's gate. As he lay there suffering, stray dogs from the street came to lick his sores. But the rich man did not try to help him at all; he let him lie there day after day in his misery.

"By and by the poor beggar died, and the angels came and carried him to heaven. No longer was he a

THE BEGGAR AT THE RICH MAN'S GATE

poor beggar, for now he could rest in peace and happiness with faithful Abraham and other good people who had left this world. The rich man died, too, and his friends buried him in a nice, new grave, and perhaps they mourned greatly because he had been taken away from them. But that was not the end of the rich man, for after death he found himself in a place of torment. Now he was poor, so poor that he could not even get a drink of water to cool his burning tongue.

"In this place of torment the poor rich man lifted up his eyes and saw, far, far away, the same Lazarus who used to sit at his gate and beg. He remembered Lazarus, and now he saw him resting happily with Abraham in a beautiful place. The poor rich man called loudly to Abraham and cried for mercy. He knew he could not hope to rest with Abraham in that beautiful place, but he wanted Abraham to send Lazarus with just a drop of water to cool his burning tongue.

"But Abraham called back that he could send no water. He said, 'Remember that you enjoyed good things in your lifetime, while Lazarus had only poverty and suffering when he lived in the world. Now he is comforted, and you are being tormented. And I can send nothing to you because no one can pass from this place to your place of torment, neither can anyone from your place come to us.'

"Now the poor rich man remembered his brothers who were yet living in the world. He did not want them to come to the place of torment, and he asked Abraham to send Lazarus back to the world to warn his brothers about that dreadful place. But Abraham said those brothers had God's law to warn them, and Lazarus need not go. Then the poor rich man pleaded that his brothers might listen if someone rose from the dead to tell them about the place of torment. But Abraham answered, 'If they will not hear the words in God's Book, neither will they listen if one should rise from the dead and speak to them.' "

Questions and Answers

1. How does God judge people? (By their hearts.)
2. What story did Jesus tell that proves this? (The story of the rich man and Lazarus.)
3. What happened to them after they died? (The beggar was happy in heaven, but the rich man was begging for water.)

STORY 47

Happenings on the Way to Jerusalem

Matt. 20:17-34; Mark 10:32-52; Luke 18:31-43

The time had come again for the Passover Feast at Jerusalem, and Jesus knew that his life on earth would soon be ended. He took his twelve disciples aside from the crowd which followed and told them again that soon he should be given into the hands of the chief priests and the scribes, his enemies, and be condemned to die. But the disciples could not understand; for they believed surely he was the Son of God and that he would become the king of the Jews.

Two of his disciples, James and John, came to him soon afterwards, bringing their mother. She knelt before Jesus and asked him to grant places of honor to her sons when he received his kingdom. Jesus knew these disciples and their mother did not understand that the kingdom of heaven would not be like an earthly kingdom, and he said that places of honor would be given only by God the Father.

The other disciples felt jealous of these two, and Jesus knew about their feelings. He called them aside again and told them that in his kingdom those who would be

JESUS TALKING WITH JAMES AND JOHN'S MOTHER

great must be the servants of all the others. He reminded them of how he had labored hard and long for others, and he told them that they should serve others too.

Many other people were going to Jerusalem to attend the Feast, and they walked along the roadway with Jesus and his disciples. These people had heard Jesus teach, and they had seen him heal the sick. They, too, hoped that he would set up his kingdom in Jerusalem.

By and by the multitude came to a city called Jericho. The road to Jerusalem led through the streets of this city, and soon the people of Jericho were much excited because Jesus was with them. News of his coming spread rapidly from one part of town to another, and many who had heard of Jesus came rushing to see him.

A blind man named Bartimaeus sat by the roadside begging. He heard the sound of many footsteps, and he wondered why such a crowd was passing, so he asked the reason. And someone answered, "Jesus of Nazareth is going by."

Bartimaeus had heard about Jesus of Nazareth. He had probably heard about the man who had been born blind and who had been healed by this wonderful man from Nazareth in Galilee. Now he wished that Jesus would have mercy on him too. He rose from his seat by the roadside and began to cry loudly, "Jesus, son of David, have mercy on me!"

Those who stood by were displeased to hear the blind beggar crying after Jesus in this way. They told him to

JESUS HEALING BARTIMAEUS

keep quiet. Perhaps they said that Jesus could not hear him; for the noise of the crowd was great. But Bartimaeus would not be quieted. He cried louder than ever; for he wished to have Jesus heal his blinded eyes.

Jesus heard the poor beggar, and he knew how the men near by had urged him to keep still. He stopped and commanded someone to tell the blind man to come to him. A messenger hurried to Bartimaeus, saying, "Be of good comfort, for Jesus has heard you and now he is calling for you."

Bartimaeus threw aside his garment and ran eagerly to the place where Jesus stood. Jesus asked, "What do you wish me to do for you?"

"Lord, give me my sight," he asked.

Jesus answered, "Go your way; your faith in me has made you well."

At once the blind eyes opened, and Bartimaeus could see as well as those who had never been blind. And he joined the crowd to follow Jesus.

Questions and Answers

1. What request did the mother of James and John make of Jesus? (She asked Jesus to give her sons the best places in his kingdom.)

2. When Jesus came to Jericho, who called to him? (A man named Bartimaeus.)

3. What did Jesus do when he heard someone calling him? (He commanded that the blind man be brought to him.)

4. How did Bartimaeus please Jesus? (By believing that Jesus could heal him.)

STORY 48

A Little Man Climbs a Tree to See Jesus

Luke 19:1-28

There was living in Jericho at the time a rich man named Zacchaeus, and he was chief among the publicans. He had never seen Jesus, and when the news came that Jesus was passing through Jericho on his way to attend the Passover Feast in Jerusalem, Zacchaeus determined that he would try to see this wonderful man. So down to the highway Zacchaeus went, hurrying along with the gathering crowd, for Jesus was to pass that way.

But Zacchaeus did not stop when the crowd stood still. He hurried a little farther on, and there he climbed into a sycamore tree that grew by the roadside. From this place he knew he could surely see Jesus when he passed by. If he had remained in the crowd he could not have seen the wonderful man from Galilee, for Zacchaeus was not so tall as the other people about him.

Soon the travelers bound for Jerusalem came down the road, and the people of Jericho, who had gathered to watch them pass, looked eagerly to catch a glimpse of Jesus. On the travelers went till they came to the sycamore tree. Here Jesus and his disciples stood still. Then

JESUS WITH ZACCHAEUS

Jesus looked up into the tree and saw Zacchaeus clinging to its branches and looking down upon him.

"Zacchaeus," said Jesus, "come down at once, for today I must stop at your house."

How surprised Zacchaeus was to hear these words! He had hoped to catch at least a glimpse of Jesus. Now he could take this wonderful man into his home and talk face to face with him.

With a joyful heart Zacchaeus led the way to his home, to entertain Jesus and his disciples there. And as they went, others followed, some finding fault because Jesus was going to stop in the home of a publican, whom they called a sinful man. The Pharisees would not enter such a house, for they despised people they called sinners and would not be friendly with them.

Although Zacchaeus was a publican, his heart had been changed by the kind words of Jesus. So he stood up before Jesus and said, "Behold, Lord, I give half of my goods to the poor, and if I have in my business dealings taken more from any man than I should have taken, I give him back four times as much as I took from him."

Jesus was pleased with Zacchaeus; for he knew this publican really had been changed in his heart. And he said, "Today salvation is come to your house, for the Son of Man is come to seek and to save those who are lost." He had known about this publican who longed to see him, and he had sought for Zacchaeus. Now he would grant him forgiveness, because Zacchaeus had received him gladly and had confessed his willingness to make his wrongs right.

Others stood by listening, and Jesus took this time to give them another parable, or story sermon. He knew the people were expecting the kingdom of heaven to be set up soon like an earthly kingdom, so he told them this story about what the kingdom of heaven is like.

"A certain nobleman went away to a far country to receive for himself a kingdom and to be made the ruler of it. Before leaving home he gave a sum of money, called a pound, to each of his ten servants, and commanded them to use the money till his return.

"After some time the nobleman came back again, having received the crown and the kingdom in that far-away country. Then he called his ten servants and asked them how they had used the money he had given to them before he went away.

"The first servant came to him bringing ten pieces of money, and saying, 'I traded with the pound you gave me, and I have gained these ten pounds.'

"The nobleman was pleased with that servant and said to him, 'Because you have done this, I will give you the rule of ten cities in my kingdom.'

"Next came a servant who had gained five pounds by using the money the nobleman had given him. And the nobleman was pleased with him also, and said, 'To you I will give the rule of five cities in the kingdom which I have received.'

"Then came the third servant, bringing only one pound, the same one that the nobleman had given him before he went away. 'Here is your pound,' the servant said, 'I have kept it wrapped in this napkin all the while you were away for fear I might lose it. I know you are a harsh master, taking up what you do not lay down and reaping what you do not sow.'

"With this servant the nobleman was much displeased. He answered, 'If you know I am a harsh master, why did you not put my money into a bank that I might have it and its gains at my return?' He commanded those who stood by to take the one pound away from the unfaithful servant and give it to the one having ten pounds.

"The servants were surprised, and they said, 'Lord, he has ten pounds, why give him more?'

"The nobleman answered, 'To every one who uses what he has, more shall be given; but those who refuse to use what is given to them shall have their own taken away.' "

Questions and Answers

1. Why did Zacchaeus climb into a tree when he heard that Jesus was passing? (He was not very tall and wanted to be sure to see Jesus.)
2. What did Jesus say when he saw Zacchaeus? ("Come down; I must stop at your house today.")
3. How may we know that Zacchaeus was pleased to have Jesus visit his home? (He received him gladly and promised to make his wrongs right.)
4. What great blessing did Jesus bring to that home? (Salvation.)

STORY 49

Mary Shows Her Love for Jesus

Matt. 26:6-16; Mark 14:3-11; John 12:1-11

"Simon the leper" was a friend of Jesus. He lived in the village of Bethany, not far from the home of Martha, Mary, and their brother Lazarus. But "Simon the leper" was no longer a leper, for Jesus had made him well of that disease. No wonder Simon was a friend of Jesus!

News reached the village of Bethany that Jesus and his disciples were coming over the road from Jericho and would soon arrive. This was glad news to the friends who loved him so dearly, and they began to plan at once how they might give him a welcome. "Simon the leper" arranged to make a supper at his home for the tired guests, and Martha, the sister of Lazarus, went to help prepare and serve the evening meal.

At last the guests arrived, and they were welcomed at the home of Simon. Then the food was placed on the table and the guests were brought into the dining hall. Curious onlookers crowded in, for news of this supper had spread quickly through the village, and even as far as Jerusalem. And uninvited persons had come, not only to see Jesus, but also to see Lazarus, whom Jesus had called out of the grave after he had been dead four days.

While the guests were eating, presently Mary arrived with a box in her hand. Going directly to the couch where Jesus was reclining, she broke the box and poured costly perfume upon Jesus' head and feet. Mary poured it all upon the body of Jesus to show her love for him. Then she bent low and wiped the feet of Jesus with her long hair.

Just as soon as the box was broken the odor of the sweet perfume filled the room. And everyone present knew this perfume had cost much money, for it was of the very best kind. At once the disciples began to whisper among themselves about what Mary had done. One of them, Judas Iscariot, who carried the moneybag for Jesus and the other disciples, became angry and said, "What a waste of money this foolish woman has made! Instead of pouring it all upon Jesus she might have given that money to buy food for the poor."

Jesus knew the thoughts and whisperings of his disciples. He saw them question Mary about her deed, and speak unkindly to her. So he spoke to them all and said, "Let this woman alone. Why do you trouble her? She has done a good work, for she has come before my death to anoint my body with sweet perfume. The poor you have with you always, but I shall not be with you much longer. By this deed Mary has shown her love for me."

Perhaps Mary understood what the disciples were unable to believe—that Jesus soon must die—for she had sat at his feet and listened to his words while he

LOOSING THE COLT

JESUS RIDING INTO JERUSALEM

visited in her home. She had heard him tell about many things, and she had believed them. And now she had poured out a costly gift to anoint Jesus.

Judas Iscariot was even more displeased when he heard Jesus' words. He was no longer a true disciple, for he had allowed Satan to plant wrong desires in his heart. Sometimes he took money from the bag for himself, for he loved riches. He had hoped some day to be a rich ruler in the kingdom he expected Jesus to set up.

Now a wicked thought crept into his heart, and he planned to go as soon as possible to the enemies of Jesus in Jerusalem and promise them to give Jesus into their power if they would give him money for his work. After the supper was ended he left Bethany and went to see the chief priests and scribes who lived in Jerusalem.

For many days the enemies of Jesus had been talking together about how they might capture Jesus. When Judas Iscariot came to them they were glad, and they promised to give him thirty pieces of silver money if he would bring them to Jesus.

Questions and Answers

1. When Jesus came to Bethany, who made a supper for him? (Simon the leper.)

2. How did Mary show her great love for Jesus at this supper? (She anointed Jesus' head and feet with expensive ointment.)

3. Who found fault with Mary? (The disciples, especially Judas Iscariot.)

4. On what wicked errand did Judas Iscariot go after supper? (He went to the enemies of Jesus and promised to betray Jesus for money.)

STORY 50

Jesus Rides into Jerusalem as a King

Matt. 21:1-11; Mark 11:1-11; Luke 19:29-40; John 12:12-19

There was great excitement. People were flocking out of the city gate and hurrying along the road that led down the valley and up the slope of Mount Olivet, just outside of Jerusalem. They were rushing out to meet Jesus, of whom they had heard such great things.

Many of these people were strangers in Jerusalem. They had just come to attend the Feast of the Passover, and they had heard about the wonderful miracles Jesus performed. As they went they took branches of palm trees with which to wave him a welcome when they should meet him.

On the morning of that same day Jesus had sent two of his disciples to a village near Bethany to loose a colt which they should find tied. He had told them to bring this colt to him, and if the owners should question why they untied the colt they should answer, "The Lord has need of this colt today." The disciples had gone, had found the colt tied by the roadside, and had given the owners Jesus' message. And the owners had let them take the colt and bring it to Jesus.

The disciples had spread their garments on the colt's

"HOSANNA!"

back and had set Jesus on it. Others threw their clothes along the road for Jesus to ride over. And as the crowd from Jerusalem came near to the Mount of Olives, the company which followed from Bethany began to shout, "Blessed is the King who is coming in the name of the Lord! Peace in heaven, and glory in the highest!"

The people who came out of Jerusalem met Jesus and his disciples on the slope of the Mount of Olives. They heard those who followed Jesus shout praises to him, and they, too, rejoiced and waved their palms, saying, "Hosanna! Blessed is the King of Israel who comes in the name of the Lord!" Some threw their palms in the road for him to ride over. All along the highway people stood, rejoicing greatly and praising God.

In the crowd were some Pharisees who had not come to rejoice, but to find fault. When they heard the people shouting they came to Jesus and said, "Master, cause these to cease shouting."

Jesus answered, "If these should be still, the stones by the roadside would immediately cry out." Jesus knew the time had come when the prophecy of Zechariah should be fulfilled:

> "Rejoice greatly, O daughter of Zion;
> Shout, O daughter of Jerusalem:
> Behold, your King comes unto you:
> He is just, and having salvation;
> Lowly, and riding upon a colt."

CHILDREN HONORING JESUS IN THE TEMPLE

So the crowd passed on through the gate into the city, and Jesus rode up Mount Moriah, where the Temple stood. And as he went, the people before and behind cried out aloud, "Hosanna to the Son of David." And the people in the city were stirred with the excitement. They came hurrying into the streets to ask, "What is the meaning of all this? Who is this king you are bringing?" And the multitude answered, "This is Jesus, the prophet of Nazareth, of Galilee."

Jesus entered the Temple and looked upon the things there. Taking his disciples, he returned to Bethany to spend the night in the house of his friends.

Questions and Answers

1. Why did Jesus have to borrow a colt on which to ride into Jerusalem? (Neither he nor his disciples owned one.)
2. Whom did he send to borrow the colt? (Two of the disciples.)
3. How did the disciples and friends of Jesus show their pleasure as he rode towards the city? (They spread their coats and palm branches on the ground for him to ride over.)
4. Who found fault when the people praised God? (The Pharisees.)

STORY 51

Jesus Teaches in the Temple

Matt. 21:12-46; Mark 11:12—12:12; Luke 19:41—20:19

Early in the morning Jesus and his disciples started away from Bethany to go again to the Temple in Jerusalem. When Jesus came to the Temple he saw men in there who were buying and selling animals for sacrifice offerings, and others who were called money-changers. Once before he had driven such men out of the Temple, and now he drove them out the second time, saying, "In the Scriptures it is written, 'My house shall be called a house of prayer'; but you have made it a den of thieves." These men demanded more money for their sacrifice offerings than they should have asked.

The wave of excitement was still running high in the city, and everyone was eager to see Jesus. The blind and the lame came to him in the Temple, and he healed them there. Children came singing, "Hosanna to the Son of David!" They had heard the glad songs of the grown people who had come with Jesus from the Mount of Olives, and they, too, wished to praise this great man, who took little ones in his arms and blessed them.

The chief priests and scribes in the Temple saw Jesus heal the blind and the lame, and they heard the children sing his praises. They were angered by these things, for they saw that every day the multitudes were becoming more excited about this Jesus. They came to him and asked, "Do you hear what these children are saying?"

Jesus replied, "Yes, I hear them. Have you never read these words in the Scriptures, 'Out of the mouths of little children thou hast perfected praise'?"

In the evening Jesus returned again with his disciples to Bethany, to be with his dear friends, and in the morning he went back to teach the eager people who gathered early to hear him.

When they came to the Temple many people had already gathered to hear Jesus teach. The chief priests and the scribes were there also, ready to ask him a question; for they were not willing that he should teach the people. They demanded of him, "By what authority do you teach and work miracles? Who gave you this authority?"

Jesus knew how to answer them by asking a question of them. He said, "Was the baptism of John from heaven or of men? Tell me this and I will answer your question."

Now the enemies of Jesus did not know how to answer. They had not received John's baptism as of God, and they feared to tell Jesus because many people were listening, and all the people claimed that surely John was a prophet of God. If they should not own John as a prophet, they feared that the people would turn bitterly against them. Yet if they should say that John's baptism

JESUS TEACHING IN THE TEMPLE

PREPARING THE LAST SUPPER

was of God, they knew Jesus would ask why they had not believed him. So they said, "We cannot tell whether John's baptism was from heaven or of men."

Then Jesus answered, "Neither will I tell you by what authority I do these things, or who gave this authority to me."

Again Jesus began to teach by story sermons, called parables. He told about a man who had two sons. This man called his elder son to him and said, "Son, go and work today in my vineyard." The boy answered his father roughly, saying, "I will not go!" But afterwards he became sorry, and repented of his unwillingness to obey his father's command. Then he went to the vineyard and worked. To the second son the father spoke the same words of command, and this boy replied politely, "I go, sir." But he did not go. "Now," asked Jesus, "which of the two boys obeyed his father?" and the people answered, "The first."

Jesus said the two boys were like the two classes—the people whom the Pharisees called sinners, and the Pharisees and other leaders themselves. All these leaders claimed to be obedient, and yet they were not doing the things God had commanded; while the other people, whom they called sinners, had listened gladly to John's words and had been baptized by him.

Another story which Jesus told was about a man who planted a vineyard, and built a hedge about it, digged a wine press in it, and built a watchtower. Then he hired some men to care for it, and went away to another country. When the time came for the fruit of the vineyard to be ripe, he sent servants to get some of the fruit and bring it back to him. But the keepers of the vineyard treated the servants roughly. The first one who came they beat, and sent him away without any fruit. The second one they threw stones at and wounded him in the head. The third one they killed. Later, other servants were sent; but the wicked keepers of the vineyard treated them all shamefully.

The owner of the vineyard was very sad, and he decided at last to send his own son. "They will know he is my son," he reasoned, "and they will respect him."

But when the keepers looked out from the watchtower and saw the son coming, they said to each other, "The owner has sent his son. This vineyard will belong to him, because he is the heir. Let us kill him, and take the vineyard for our own possession."

They caught him, and killed him, and threw his body outside the vineyard.

"When the owner of that vineyard comes, what will he do to those men?" asked Jesus.

And the people answered, "He will cause them to be miserably destroyed, and he will give his vineyard into the care of better men, who will give him some of its fruits."

Then Jesus looked boldly upon his enemies standing near and said, "The kingdom of God shall be taken from you, and shall be given to another nation, which will bring forth fruit."

The chief priests and scribes knew he had spoken the parables against them, and they were angry. But they were afraid to seize him, because they knew all the people standing round believed that Jesus was a great prophet.

Questions and Answers

1. How did the children in the Temple please Jesus? (They sang, calling Jesus the Son of David.)

2. Why would not Jesus' enemies tell him what they thought about John's baptism? (They were afraid to offend the listening people, who believed that John was a prophet.)

3. Why, in the story which Jesus told, did the owner send his son to bring fruit from his vineyard? (Because the keepers of the vineyard had killed the servants whom he sent.)

4. Why were the chief priests and scribes angry when they heard this parable? (They knew it was spoken against them.)

STORY 52

Jesus' Last Days in the Temple

Matt. 22:1—24: 1; Mark 12:13—13:1; Luke 20:20—21:4; John 12:20-36

While Jesus was teaching in the Temple he told the people by a parable that the kingdom of heaven is like a king who made a feast at the marriage of his son. The king prepared a great feast and invited guests from a near-by city. When everything was ready, the guests failed to come. He sent servants to remind them of their invitation to the wedding feast; still they would not come. They made fun of it, and went on about their own work. Some of them even treated the king's messengers cruelly and killed them.

The king heard about the conduct of those people, and he was much displeased. He called out his army and sent his soldiers to destroy them and to burn their city. Then he invited other guests to the marriage feast, and the place was filled; for this time every one bidden came.

Among these guests were the poor and the rich, and the good and the bad, and the king furnished each one with a garment to wear. He wished to have them appear well in his presence. When all had arrived and put on their clean garments, he came in to see them and to give them a welcome to the feast.

One man was present who refused to put on the clean garment that the king had provided for him. There he stood among all the others, clothed in his dirty rags. The king saw him and said, "Friend, why did you come in here without putting on the clean garment that I had provided for you to wear?"

The man hung his head, for he had no excuse to offer. The king was displeased with him because he had disobeyed orders, so he commanded his servants to seize the man, bind him hand and foot, and take him away.

The Pharisees and other enemies of Jesus knew these parables were showing how they had refused to obey God, and they determined to put a stop to his teaching. They decided to ask questions of him, to prevent this kind of teaching. They sent some men who pretended to be good, and told these men to ask him whether it was wrong or right to pay the tribute money, or tax money, which Caesar, the Roman ruler, demanded of them.

The Jews disliked to pay this money, and Jesus' enemies knew that if he would say it was right for them to pay the tax, then the people would no longer care to make him their king. They would no longer follow him so eagerly and listen to his words, for they hated the Roman government. But if Jesus would say it was wrong to pay this tax money, then his enemies planned to tell the Roman officers that Jesus was unwilling to obey the Roman government, and they knew Jesus would be punished.

The men came to Jesus and said, "Master, we know you are true, and that you teach the way of God in truth without caring whether men will be pleased with your teaching or not." Thus they flattered him, thinking he would be delighted to hear such favorable things said of himself. Then they continued: "Tell us just what you think, Is it right or wrong to pay this tribute money which Caesar demands of us Jews?" They thought Jesus would answer either yes or no. But they were mistaken.

Jesus could see the hearts of these evil men who were questioning him. He paid no attention to their flattering words, but said, "Why do you tempt me, you hypocrites? Show me the tribute money."

They brought him a penny. Jesus looked at the coin on both sides, then asked of them, "Whose image is this on the one side? and whose name is written here?" On one side of the coin was a picture of Caesar's head, and his name was written above it.

The men replied that the image and the name on the coin were both Caesar's.

"Then," said Jesus, "give to Caesar the things that belong to him, and give to God the things that belong to God."

This answer greatly surprised the men, for they had thought they surely would catch Jesus in a trap where he would need to say yes or no. But he had replied so wisely they could not accuse him to any man.

Others came to question Jesus, and among them was a lawyer who asked, "Which is the greatest commandment of the law?"

Jesus replied that the greatest commandment of the law was, "Thou shalt love the Lord thy God with all thy heart, and with all thy soul, and with all thy mind, and with all thy strength: this is the first commandment. And the second greatest is this: Thou shalt love thy neighbor as much as thyself. No other commandments are so important as these two."

The lawyer answered, "You have well spoken, for to love the Lord God in this way and to love one's neighbor as much as one's own self is surely more pleasing to God than burnt offerings and sacrifices."

Jesus was pleased with this reply of the lawyer. He saw that the lawyer understood the meaning of God's Word better than many who pretended to be teachers of it. And he told the lawyer that he was near to the kingdom of God.

While Jesus was in the Temple, some men came to Philip, one of the twelve disciples, and asked permission to see Jesus. These men were Gentiles, Greeks by birth, and they had come to worship the God of the Jews. Because they were Gentiles they could not enter the part of the Temple where Jesus sat teaching the people who thronged him there. They could come no farther than the outside court, called the court of the Gentiles. But they had heard much about this wonderful teacher from

Galilee, and they wished to see him. Philip told Andrew, another disciple, and together they hurried to tell Jesus that strangers from Greece, a country far away, were waiting in the court of the Gentiles to see him.

When Jesus heard about the inquirers from distant Greece he said to Philip and Andrew, "The hour is come that the Son of Man should be glorified." He spoke to them about his coming death for the sins of the people, but the disciples could not understand his words. And because Jesus could feel pain just as we do, he shrank from the thought of dying on the cross. He felt troubled because the time was drawing so near when he should die. And he said, prayerfully, "Father, save me from this hour." Then he remembered that his lifework would not be finished if he did not die for lost sinners, so he added, "Father, glorify thy name."

Then a voice spoke from heaven, "I have glorified it, and will glorify it again." The people standing by heard the voice but could not understand the words that were spoken. Some thought the voice sounded like thunder; others said, "An angel spoke to him." But Jesus said the voice had spoken to prove to them that God had heard him.

After teaching, Jesus had sat down near a place in the Temple called the treasury. Here were money boxes in which the people's offerings were received. Jesus saw the rich pass by the boxes and throw in large offerings. He saw a poor widow come into the treasury and stop

WIDOW DROPPING IN HER OFFERING

beside a box to throw in her small offering of only two little coins. Together these coins were worth less than a penny. But Jesus told his disciples that the poor widow had given more than the rich people, for they had given out of full purses whereas she had emptied the last of her money into the box. He wished to teach them that God looks at the heart of the giver, for God saw that the poor widow gave her all because she loved him, whereas the rich people gave their offerings because it was their duty to give.

Then Jesus and his disciples left the Temple and went out to the Mount of Olives. Never again did Jesus walk in the courts of the Lord's house on Mount Moriah, for soon afterwards his enemies took him.

Questions and Answers

1. Why did Jesus' enemies ask him if it was right to pay taxes to the Romans? (They hoped his answer would get him into trouble.)
2. From what country had the Gentile strangers come, who asked to see Jesus? (From Greece.)
3. Why was Jesus troubled at this time? (He knew the time was near when he should suffer and die on the cross.)
4. What did Jesus say about the poor widow's offering which she threw into the Temple treasury? (He said that her small offering was more in God's sight than the large offerings of the rich.)

STORY 53

Jesus Teaches on the Mount of Olives

Matt. 23:37—25:46; Mark 13; Luke 21:5-38

As Jesus left the Temple for the last time his disciples spoke to him about the beauty of the Lord's house. Like all other Jews, they took much pride in the Temple where God was worshiped. And they were surprised to hear Jesus say, "The time is coming when the stones of these buildings shall be torn apart."

On the Mount of Olives Jesus rested for a while before going on to Bethany. And his disciples gathered around him there to ask when the time should come that the beautiful Temple would be destroyed. No one else was near to disturb them, and Jesus talked long and earnestly to his disciples about the things that would happen to Jerusalem, and later to the whole world. He told them that men would come who would claim to be the Christ of God, and that many would believe in them. He said that great wars would be fought among the nations of the earth, and that troubles of different kinds would come upon the people. He said that before the end of time the gospel of the kingdom would be preached, not only among the Jews, but to all people in every part of the world. How strange these things must have sounded to the disciples, who had always believed that salvation belonged to the Jews only!

Then Jesus told the disciples the parable of the ten young women, called virgins. Five of these young women were wise and five were foolish. All had been invited to the marriage of a friend, and they started to meet the wedding party. They took their lamps with them to give light, for the wedding would take place at night and only those carrying lights would be allowed to join the wedding party.

But the wedding party was slow in coming, and the young women grew tired waiting and fell asleep. At midnight a cry was made that the wedding party was coming, and the young women aroused and began at once to trim their lamps to be ready to join the procession when it came by.

Now the five who were wise poured more oil into their lamps, for they saw the light was growing dim. They had brought an extra supply of oil with them. The five who were foolish had brought no more oil, and they, too, saw that their lights were growing dim. "What shall we do?" they asked each other. Then they spoke to their wise friends and said, "Please give some of your oil to us, for our lights are going out!"

The wise young women did not have enough to give to their friends in distress, so they answered, "You must go to them who sell and buy for yourselves. We do not have enough to share." While they hurried away to buy more oil, the wedding party came, and the five wise young women joined the party and went to the home where the marriage festivities would take place.

When all the guests had entered, the door was shut, and no other persons could enter. The foolish young women came after the door had been shut, and they knocked; but the bridegroom would not let them in. They had come too late.

By this story Jesus wished to teach his disciples to watch and to be ready, for they could not know the time when he would call for them to leave this world and go to be with him. If they were not ready when he called, they would have no time left in which to get ready, but, like the foolish young women, they would be shut out of heaven.

Jesus told the disciples what will happen at the end of the world. He said that then the Son of Man will come in his glory, bringing all the angels with him. He will sit upon the throne of his glory. Before him all nations of the earth shall be gathered, and he will divide the good from the evil. Those who have believed in him he will place on his right, and those who have disobeyed he will place on his left, just as a shepherd in that country divided his sheep from his goats. Perhaps the disciples had watched the shepherds separate the sheep from the goats in their great flocks, and they understood how this separation will be.

JESUS AND HIS DISCIPLES

"Then shall the Son of Man be King," said Jesus, "and he will say to them on his right, 'Come, you who are blessed of my Father, and dwell in the kingdom which has been prepared for you. For I was hungry, and you fed me; I was thirsty and you gave me drink; I was a stranger, and you gave me shelter; I was shivering with cold, and you gave me clothes to keep me warm; I was sick, and you visited me; I was in prison, and you came to see me even there.'

"And the ones on his right will reply, 'Lord, when did we see you in need and help you thus?'

"And the King will answer, 'Whenever you helped one of my needy brothers, even the least of them, you helped me.'

"Then the King will turn to those on his left, and will say to them, 'Depart from me, you who are cursed, and go away into everlasting fire, which has been made ready for the devil and his evil spirits. For I was hungry, and you did not feed me; I was thirsty, and you gave me no water; I was a stranger, and you gave me no shelter; without clothes, and you did not give clothes to me; sick, and you did not visit me; in prison, and you did not come to me there.'

"And the ones on his left will reply, 'Lord, when did we see you hungry, or thirsty, or without clothes, or a stranger, or sick, or in prison, and not help you?' And he will say to them, 'Whenever you refused to help one of my brothers, even the poorest of them, you refused to help me.'

"And those on the right," said Jesus, "will go into life eternal in heaven, while those on the left shall be turned away into everlasting torment."

Questions and Answers

1. What did the disciples ask Jesus about the beautiful Temple? (They asked when the Temple would be destroyed.)

2. What were some things which Jesus said would happen before the end of time should come? (He said there would be wars, much trouble, and false teachings concerning himself.)

3. What did Jesus wish to teach his disciples in the Parable of the Ten Virgins? (The importance of being ready to meet the Lord.)

4. To whom did Jesus liken the sheep and the goats in his parable of the End of the World? (He likened the sheep to Christians and the goats to sinners.)

STORY 54

The Last Supper with the Twelve

Matt. 26:17-30; Mark 14:12-26; Luke 22:3-39; John 13

Two disciples, Peter and John, were hurrying along the road from Bethany to Jerusalem on an errand for their master. The day had come when the lamb for the Passover feast should be killed, and Jesus had chosen these two disciples to go to Jerusalem and prepare the Feast that the Twelve would eat with him.

After they had passed through the city gate, they looked about to find a man carrying a pitcher of water. Men seldom carried water pitchers in the streets, for such work was usually left for women to do. But Jesus had told them they would see a man carrying a water pitcher, and they did. Jesus also told them to follow the man to the house where he should go with his pitcher, so they followed.

At the house they met the owner, and to him they gave the message that Jesus had sent. This was the message: "Our master sent us to ask your permission for him to use your guest room in which to eat the Passover Supper with his disciples."

The owner of the house led them to a nice room upstairs which was furnished with a table and couches

THE LAST SUPPER

on which the guests might recline while they ate. It is likely that this man knew Jesus, and was glad to give him the use of the guest room in his home for this last supper with the disciples.

When evening came Jesus and the other ten joined Peter and John, and together they sat around the table in that quiet room upstairs. A feeling of sadness crept into the hearts of the disciples, for their Master spoke to them earnestly about going away soon.

It was hard for these men to believe that Jesus would really be taken away from them. They had seen him do such wonderful things that it seemed impossible to think men ever could kill him. And soon they were talking about other matters at the supper table. Some were wondering who would be the greatest in the kingdom that they expected Jesus to set up soon. They were bewildered by his sayings.

Jesus knew their thoughts, and he wished to teach them more about the kind of kingdom he was bringing to mankind. He rose up suddenly from the table, laid aside his outer garment, and tied a towel about his waist. Then he took a basin of water and began to wash the disciples' feet.

The disciples looked at each other in silent astonishment. They could not understand why he should be doing this, for they had washed the dust from their feet before coming into that upper room. When Jesus came to Peter with his basin, Peter pulled his feet away, and exclaimed, "Lord, you shall never wash my feet!"

"Then," answered Jesus calmly, "you shall never have a part in my kingdom."

At this, Peter changed his mind suddenly, and he said, "Lord, you may wash my feet, and even my hands and my head."

Very desirous was this disciple of having a part in Jesus' kingdom. But by washing their feet Jesus did not mean to prepare the hearts of his disciples for his work. He said to them, "You are clean already, but not all." For he knew which one was not a true disciple.

When the strange washing was over, Jesus laid aside the towel and took up his garment again. Then he returned to his place at the table, beside John, and began to explain to his disciples what he had just done to them: "You call me Lord, and Master," said he, "and so I am. If I, your Lord and Master, have washed your feet, you ought to wash one another's feet. For I have given you an example that you should do to each other as I have done to you. The servant is not greater than his master, and if you would be good servants you will obey my words. If you know my commands, you will be happy when you obey them."

Jesus also said that one of them would give him into the hands of his enemies, who would take his life. This seemed hard to believe, but knowing that Jesus' words of prophecy always came true, the disciples were amazed. Instead of looking at each other accusingly, each man thought of himself and said, "Lord, is it I?"

John, the disciple who liked to be near Jesus, was reclining next to his master at the supper. Peter motioned to John and whispered, "Ask which one will do this dreadful deed."

John asked Jesus, and Jesus replied in low tones, "The one to whom I shall give a piece of bread when I have dipped it in the dish." John watched carefully, and soon he saw Jesus give a piece of bread to Judas Iscariot.

After Judas had taken the bread that Jesus gave to him, Jesus said, "That thou doest, do quickly." Then Judas hurried out of the room into the gloom of night. None of the disciples understood what Jesus meant, but they supposed that because Judas carried the moneybag he was going to do something for their master.

Jesus then, after supper, took bread and blessed it and broke it in pieces, giving parts to each of the disciples, and saying, "Take this bread and eat it, for it is my body which is broken for you." Then he took the cup, and when he had given thanks he passed it to them, saying, "Drink this, for it is my blood, which is shed for you, for I will never again drink of the fruit of the vine with you until that day when I drink it new in the kingdom of God."

They lingered awhile longer in the upper room, and

JESUS AND HIS DISCIPLES LEAVING FOR GETHSEMANE

Jesus talked earnestly to them about the time when he should go away and leave them alone. He urged them to remember his commandment to love each other as he had loved them, and he told them that he would prepare a place for them in his Father's house.

Peter insisted that he would not leave Jesus, but would go with him wherever he went. Jesus told him that he could not go now, but that he might come later on. He also told Peter that, bold as he believed himself to be, he would prove himself a coward before daylight should return, for he would forsake Jesus and even deny that he had ever known him. Then Jesus and his disciples sang a hymn together, quietly left the upper room, and went out of Jerusalem into a garden near by.

Questions and Answers

1. On what errand to Jerusalem did Jesus send Peter and John? (To prepare their Passover feast.)
2. What strange example of humility did Jesus set before his disciples? (He washed their feet and dried them with a towel.)
3. By what sign did Jesus tell John which of the Twelve should betray him? (By giving to the guilty one a piece of bread.)
4. What did Jesus do with bread and wine after supper had ended? (He blessed the bread and wine and gave it to his disciples.)

STORY 55

An Untrue Disciple Sells His Lord

Matt. 26:36-75; Mark 14:32-72; Luke 22:39-71; John 18:1-27

Through the deep shadows which fell from the buildings along the streets a silent figure glided along, hurrying toward the assembly room where the enemies of Jesus were sitting together waiting. That silent figure was Judas Iscariot, who was hurrying on his way to sell his Lord.

Soon the footsteps of Judas fell on the floor of the hall, and his knock sounded on the door of the assembly room. In reply to the call, "Who is there?" came the answer, "He for whom you wait," and quickly the door was thrown open and Judas entered. Now there followed a hasty conversation, some argument, and finally thirty pieces of silver were counted out and handed to Judas. Then the assembly broke up, each man hurrying to get a torch or to summon the soldiers who should go on their midnight errand.

This was taking place while Jesus and the eleven disciples were going to the garden across the brook Kidron. Here at the entrance of the garden Jesus had told eight of the disciples to wait and, taking with him Peter,

PETER PRETENDING NOT TO KNOW JESUS

THE CRUCIFIXION

James, and John, he had gone into the deeper shadows of the trees to pray.

While Jesus prayed the disciples fell asleep. They could not understand why he should seem so troubled, and they did not know how to comfort him. They allowed their own sleepy feelings to overcome their love for him, and just when he longed to have them near to pray with him they slept. Three times Jesus went to waken Peter, James, and John, but not once did they offer him the comfort he sought. Then while he prayed in agony alone, God sent an angel from heaven to strengthen and comfort him. Jesus knew the sorrow that was soon to come; he knew what Judas was even then doing; and he knew his enemies would not cease to torture him till he should be hanging dead upon the cross. Not only that, for Jesus knew also that he must bear the sins of the whole world in order to become the Savior of men. And because he had a body like ours, he dreaded to suffer the pain of such a death, and he dreaded to be left alone by those whom he loved. So he asked God to take away the suffering from him if such a thing could be possible. But he added, "Let thy will, not mine, be done."

When Jesus had roused the sleepy disciples the third time, he told them to arise, for it was time for them to be going on their way. And they rose up to follow him out of the garden. But as they went toward the entrance they saw a band of men coming to them carrying torches

JESUS PRAYING IN THE GARDEN

as if they were searching for someone. Jesus walked up to the men and asked, "For whom are you seeking?"

They replied, "For Jesus of Nazareth."

"I am he," answered Jesus.

And the men fell backward. When they rose, Jesus asked them the second time whom they were seeking, and again they said, "Jesus of Nazareth."

Judas, the unfaithful disciple, was with the band of men, and he stepped forward and cried, "Hail, Master!" and kissed Jesus on the cheek.

Jesus knew the evil thought that was in Judas' mind, and he looked sadly into the guilty face of his unfaithful disciple and asked, "Judas, do you betray the Son of Man with a kiss?"

Judas had told the band of men the sign by which they might know whom to take for their prisoner, and that sign was the kiss he had given to Jesus. Now the soldiers took hold of Jesus roughly to lead him away.

At this Peter was thoroughly aroused from his sleep. Drawing a short sword, which he carried in his belt, he struck at one of the soldiers and cut off his ear. But Jesus seemed displeased, and told Peter to put away his sword. Then he healed the soldier's ear. Peter, unable to understand how he might now defend his master, sank back into the shadows with the other frightened disciples.

The soldiers then bound their prisoner, and the procession started toward the assembly room where the enemies of Jesus were waiting impatiently. Peter followed far behind, wondering what he should do and yet fearing that the soldiers might take him as they had taken Jesus.

The soldiers brought Jesus to the house of a man named Annas, who was father-in-law of the high priest, Caiaphas, and here his trial began. John, one of the disciples, gained admittance at the door, for he was acquainted with the household of the high priest. And he went in where Jesus was. But Peter stood outside, for he was a stranger, and the doorkeeper, a young girl, would not let him in.

Presently John spoke to the doorkeeper, and she allowed him to take Peter into the courtroom, for the night was cold. When Peter was inside the young girl said, "Are you not also one of his disciples?" Peter was afraid, and he said, "No, I do not know the man."

In the open court a fire was burning, and Peter went near to warm himself. Around the fire stood other men, some who were servants in the high priest's house and others who were officers.

One of the men by the fire then turned to Peter and asked, "Are you not one of this man's disciples?" Again fear crept into Peter's heart, and he replied stoutly, "No, I am not!"

A soldier standing by who had been in the garden when Jesus was taken had seen Peter use his sword, and he spoke, saying, "I saw you in the garden with him!"

Peter denied fiercely, and pretended that he had never known Jesus at all.

While this had been happening to Peter, out in the high priest's courtyard, the high priest and others had been asking Jesus questions about his teachings and had been treating him shamefully. Then the enemies of Jesus led their prisoner out of the high priest's house, and as he passed by he looked sadly upon Peter. Peter remembered how Jesus had told him that before the return of another day he would deny three times that he had ever known him. Now tears filled Peter's eyes, and he turned blindly away from the fire and rushed out of the door, to weep bitterly. He saw himself no longer a true man, brave, and ready to help in the work of his master, but a coward, ashamed to own that he had once proudly followed the innocent man who now stood bound in chains and condemned to die.

Questions and Answers

1. For how many pieces of money did Judas Iscariot sell his Lord? (Thirty.)
2. Where did Jesus and the eleven disciples go after supper? (To the garden of Gethsemane.)
3. Which of the eleven did Jesus take with him to the place of prayer? (Peter, James, and John.)
4. How did Judas, the unfaithful disciple, betray Jesus? (With a kiss.)
5. How did Peter try to defend Jesus? (He drew a sword and cut off a soldier's ear.)

STORY 56

The Darkest Day in All the World

Matt. 27:1-54; Mark 15:1-39; Luke 23:1-47; John 18:28—19:31

After the sad, long night when Jesus was captured in the garden, morning came and the news began to spread through the city streets that Jesus, the prophet from Galilee, was now a prisoner. His friends were terrified, while his enemies laughed in wicked glee. And the soldiers led him before the Roman governor, Pilate, for this governor now took the place of the King Herod who had tried to kill Jesus when he was born.

Pilate knew nothing about Jesus. He took him into his judgment hall and talked awhile with him. And he was surprised to hear the wisdom of this one whom the Jews were condemning to die. He went out to them and said, "I find no fault in this man." But the Jews cried the more loudly that Jesus should be put to death, saying that he had stirred up the people throughout the country, even from Galilee.

When Pilate heard that Jesus was from Galilee, he said, "This man belongs to the country that Herod rules." This Herod was a son of the wicked king who tried to take Jesus' life when he was a baby. Pilate

JESUS BEFORE PILATE

sent Jesus to Herod at once, for Herod was in Jerusalem at that time.

Now this was the Herod who had caused John the Baptist to be put to death. He had heard much about Jesus, but he had never seen him. When the soldiers came, bringing Jesus bound with chains, Herod was glad, for he hoped that Jesus might do some miracle before him. At once he began to ask questions of Jesus, but not one question would Jesus answer. The chief priests and the scribes stood round about and said all kinds of evil things about Jesus, still he would not speak one word to defend himself.

Finally Herod grew impatient with this silent prisoner. A wicked thought came into his heart, so he began to make fun of Jesus. With his soldiers he mocked Jesus, dressing him in rich garments and pretending to honor him as a king. Then he sent him back to Pilate.

Now Pilate's wife had heard about the trial of Jesus and she was greatly troubled, for that night she had dreamed about him. She sent a message to her husband, urging him to set Jesus free, saying, "He is a just man, not worthy of death."

Pilate, too, wished to free Jesus; for he could find no guilt in him. He told the accusers that neither he nor Herod had been able to find him guilty of death. But the mob now cried, "If you set this man free you are not a friend of Caesar, and Caesar will dismiss you from being our governor." Pilate knew the Jews could accuse him

MARY TELLING THE GOOD NEWS

JESUS' LAST MEETING WITH HIS DISCIPLES

to Caesar if they were displeased with him, and being a coward he chose rather to let an innocent man suffer than to be in danger of losing his position as governor of the province.

As the trial went on Judas Iscariot saw that Jesus was condemned to die. Now his guilty conscience troubled him greatly. He had hoped that Jesus would free himself in some miraculous way from the power of his enemies; but now he saw that Jesus was allowing himself to be helpless in their hands. The money that he had taken from the enemies of Jesus seemed to burn his flesh, so he hurried back to the chief priests and scribes, saying, "I have sold an innocent man! I have sinned!"

The chief priests and scribes looked scornfully upon Judas and replied, "What is that to us? You yourself must answer for your sin." And they turned away from him, refusing to take back the money they had given him for doing the dreadful act. Neither would Judas keep the money, so he threw it upon the floor of the Temple and ran down the long flight of steps, away to a lonely place, where he hanged himself and died.

Before giving Jesus up to die Pilate talked to the restless mob about another prisoner whom he held — a wicked man named Barabbas, who as a robber had caused much trouble to the Jews. At the time of the Feast it was customary to release a prisoner, and Pilate asked whether he should release Barabbas, the wicked robber whom the people feared, or Jesus, the innocent man whom they hated. And with loud cries the people answered, "Set Barabbas free!"

Then Pilate asked, "What shall I do with Jesus?" and they answered, "Crucify him! crucify him!"

So the trial came to an end, and Pilate, wishing to please the people, called some Roman soldiers and told them to lead Jesus away to be crucified. First he took water in a basin and washed his hands before the Jews, saying, "I am not guilty of the death of this innocent man."

The Jews cried out, "We ourselves will bear the blame; let his blood be on our heads!"

The Roman soldiers took Jesus and put a crown of thorns upon his head. Then they put a reed in his hand, and, bowing before him, mockingly called him the king of the Jews. They also blindfolded his eyes, and spat upon him, and struck him with their hands, saying, "Tell us, prophet, who is it who struck you?" All these shameful things Jesus bore in silence, for he was suffering in the place of those who deserved to suffer for their own sins. Finally the soldiers took off the purple robe and dressed him once more in his own clothes. Then they led him away outside the city to nail him on a cross. They took two other prisoners, men who had been thieves, and laid heavy crosses on the bared backs of these men, then led them away with Jesus to die.

A crowd of curious people followed the soldiers through the gate to the hillside where the crucifixion took place. Many in the crowd were enemies of Jesus, others were friends who longed to help but could not. As they went, Jesus sank down beneath the weight of the heavy cross he bore, and could not rise again. The cruel soldiers then called a stranger from the crowd and placed the cross upon his shoulder.

On the hillside of Calvary the crowd stopped, and the soldiers began to strip their prisoners of their clothing and to fasten their hands and their feet to the crosses. Then they raised the crosses high in the air and planted them securely in the ground, leaving the prisoners to hang there till death should relieve them of their misery. Jesus prayed when they were crucifying him and said, "Father, forgive them, for they know not what they do."

The cross on which Jesus was crucified stood between the two crosses on which the thieves were hung, and a writing was nailed above the head of Jesus, which said in three languages, "This is Jesus, the King of the Jews." When the Jews read the writing they were much displeased and hurried to ask Pilate to change it, that it might read thus: "He called himself the King of the Jews." But Pilate would not change the writing, and all who passed by could read what he had written.

While Jesus hung on the cross, one of the thieves began to mock him, but the other begged to be forgiven and to be remembered when Jesus came into his kingdom. He believed that Jesus was really the King from heaven, which the Jews were unwilling to receive. And Jesus saw his faith, and said to him, "Today you shall be with me in paradise." Then the thief knew that his sins were forgiven; a glad joy came into his heart.

While Jesus hung on the cross he saw a group of sorrowing friends standing at the edge of the crowd, and among them was his own mother. Jesus asked John, who was also there, to take care of his mother from that time.

The enemies of Jesus stood around the cross, making fun of him and telling him to come down if he were the Son of God. Even the chief priests and the scribes were there, and they said, "He said he could save others, but he cannot save himself! If he is the king of Israel, let him come down, and we will believe in him, too."

About noonday the sky suddenly grew dark. For three hours the great darkness lasted, then Jesus cried with a loud voice, saying, "It is finished!" and soon he died.

The Roman captain who stood near the cross said to his soldiers, "Truly this man was the Son of God!"

Questions and Answers

1. Before what Roman ruler was Jesus led as a prisoner? (Pilate.)
2. Who urged Pilate to set Jesus free? (His wife.)
3. Whom did the Jews ask to have released instead of Jesus? (Barabbas.)
4. Where was Jesus crucified? (On the hill called Calvary.)
5. What writing did Pilate cause to be nailed on the cross above the head of Jesus? ("This is Jesus, the King of the Jews.")

STORY 57

The Watchers at the Tomb

Matt. 27:55—28:1; Mark 15:42—16:5; Luke 23:50—24:1
John 19:31—20:1

The Jews who had been so gleeful when Jesus was taken prisoner and crucified still felt troubled about him. They could not put the thoughts of him out of their minds. The next day would be their Sabbath, and they did not wish to leave him hanging on the cross.

However, a rich man named Joseph, who was also a ruler among the Jews, now came boldly into Pilate's judgment hall and asked permission to take the body of Jesus and bury it. This man had loved Jesus, and he had taken no part in the wicked plots of his fellow rulers. He, with Nicodemus the Pharisee, had long believed in Jesus, but for fear of the other Jews these two men had not made known their belief. Now with Pilate's permission they went to Calvary. They took Jesus' body and wrapped it in rich linen clothes with the sweet spices and perfumes that Nicodemus the Pharisee had brought. Then they laid it in a new grave, or tomb, which had been cut out of a large rock. This grave opened into a garden, and Joseph had intended it for his own burial place when he should die.

Some of the women who had often been with Jesus when he taught the multitudes stood by watching when Joseph and Nicodemus laid the body of their beloved friend in the dark tomb, and they saw the men roll a heavy stone before the door.

Evening had now come, and the Jews' Sabbath had commenced; their Sabbath began at sunset on Friday evening and ended at sunset on Saturday evening. The sorrowing friends of Jesus therefore hastily returned to their homes to keep the Sabbath.

But the enemies of Jesus began to fear that Jesus' grave might be disturbed by his friends. They remembered that Jesus had said he would rise on the third day, and they said to each other, "His disciples may come to steal him away and then declare that he has risen. Then perhaps more people will believe in him, and we shall be despised by them." Hurrying to Pilate, they told him about their fears and asked permission to place his Roman seal upon the stone in front of Jesus' grave, and to have soldiers guard the tomb, so that no one could come by night and take away the body. Pilate allowed them to place his seal upon the great stone and to station soldiers to guard the grave by day and by night.

The women who had watched Joseph and Nicodemus lay the body of Jesus away longed to show their love for Jesus, and after sunset on the next day they hurriedly prepared some sweet perfumes. Then they planned to go early the next morning to anoint the body of their dear friend, even though he had been buried.

But the eleven disciples, stricken with sorrow, hid themselves from the scornful glances of passers-by. They had forgotten that Jesus said he would rise again on the third day. The cruel act of Judas, one of their own number, and the defenseless attitude of their master when in the hands of his enemies had so disappointed them that they bowed their heads in anguish and grief. Nothing seemed left for them now. Their glorious hopes of the kingdom of heaven had vanished like a broken bubble.

Early on the morning of the third day, before the sun had risen, a group of sorrowing women crept out of the city and sped along the highway toward the garden tomb. As they went they wondered who would roll away the stone from the door of the grave, that they might go inside and pour their sweet perfumes upon the body of Jesus. But when they came near they saw the stone was rolled away and that the tomb was empty. Other visitors had come to the tomb even earlier than they. And the body of Jesus was not there.

Questions and Answers

1. Who asked permission of Pilate to take the body of Jesus from the cross? (A rich man named Joseph.)
2. Where was the body of Jesus buried? (In Joseph's new tomb in a garden.)
3. Why did Pilate place a seal on the tomb and place a guard of soldiers there? (Jesus' enemies told Pilate that the body might be stolen.)
4. Who came to visit the tomb at early dawn the first day of the week? (A group of sorrowing women.)

THE WOMEN AT THE TOMB

STORY 58

Jesus Rises from the Dead

Matt. 28:2-16; Mark 16:5-14; Luke 24:4-12; John 20:2-18

The hours of watching dragged slowly by to the Roman soldiers who guarded the tomb where the body of Jesus lay. No one had come even to visit the grave; and perhaps the soldiers laughed at the fears of the Jews.

The eastern sky was beginning to light up with the promise of a new day, when suddenly the ground beneath the watchers' feet began to tremble. Another earthquake had come. Then the fearful watchers saw a mighty angel come down from the sky and roll the stone away from the door of the tomb and sit upon it. The face of this angel had the appearance of lightning, and the garments he wore were as white as snow. At sight of him the soldiers fell to the ground, trembling and helpless, and lay there as if they were dead. All this happened because Jesus had, in the grave, come back to life. He was risen from the dead.

When the women came to the garden they found the tomb empty, and the angel had not yet gone back to heaven. At first the women did not see the angel, and they wondered who had come and stolen the body of their Lord. Mary Magdalene left the others and ran quickly to tell Peter and John that the body of Jesus had been taken away from the tomb.

After Mary had gone from them, the other women saw the beautiful angel in the empty tomb, and they were afraid and bowed themselves to the ground. But the angel said, "Do not be afraid. Why are you seeking the living among the dead? Jesus is not here; he is risen as he said. Go quickly and tell his disciples and Peter that he is alive and will meet them in Galilee."

The women ran from the place, filled with joy, yet trembling with excitement and fear. The good news which the angel told seemed too wonderful to be true. Still, they believed and hurried to tell the disciples and other friends who were sorrowing.

But the disciples refused to believe the glad message. Peter and John ran to see the empty tomb for themselves, and when they came to the place they found no one, for the soldiers had fled into the city to tell their strange experience to the enemies of Jesus who had stationed them to watch by the grave.

John outran Peter, and coming first to the grave he looked and saw it was empty. Then Peter came, and he went into the dark room where the body of Jesus had been laid. He saw there the graveclothes that Joseph had wrapped round the body of Jesus, and he believed that surely Jesus was alive once more. John, too, entered the grave and saw the clothes lying where Jesus had left them, and he also believed.

Mary Magdalene had not stayed in the garden long enough to hear the message of the angel, and now she returned from the city, longing to find the place where her crucified Lord had been taken. She did not yet know of the new hopes that were gladdening the hearts of her friends. Entering the garden again, she stood by the empty grave and wept. Then she stooped down and looked into the grave and saw two angels sitting, one at the head and another at the foot of where the body of Jesus had been. They said to her, "Woman, why are you weeping?"

She replied, "Because they have taken away my Lord and I do not know where they have laid him." Then turning about she saw Jesus himself standing near. But tears blinded her eyes, and she did not know him. He, too, asked her why she wept, and supposing him to be the man who cared for the garden, she said, "Sir, if you have carried away my Lord, tell me where you have laid him that I may take him."

Then Jesus said, "Mary!" and she knew his voice.

What glad joy filled Mary's heart when she knew that Jesus was speaking to her again! She fell at his feet and cried, "Master!" Then he told her to go at once and tell her sorrowing friends that she had seen him and that he had told her to tell them he was going to ascend to their heavenly Father's home.

While these things were happening the soldiers came into the city and told the chief priests what had taken place in the garden tomb. And the chief priests were alarmed. They quickly called the other enemies of Jesus; and they all wondered what to do. They had no thoughts of accepting Jesus even though he had truly risen from the dead. They still hoped to persuade the people that Jesus had been a false prophet, so they decided on a plan, and they asked the soldiers to help them carry it out. They offered them much money if only they would promise to tell no one else that Jesus had risen and an angel had opened the tomb. They urged the soldiers to tell the people that the disciples came and stole Jesus' body away while they were lying asleep.

The Roman soldiers cared nothing about the Jews and their religion, and they gladly took the money and went away. And when they were questioned about the disappearance of Jesus' body from the grave, they said the disciples had stolen it while they slept.

Questions and Answers

1. Who ran to tell Peter and John that the body of Jesus had been stolen? (Mary Magdalene.)
2. What message did the other women hasten to bring to the disciples? (The glad news that Jesus had risen from the dead.)
3. Why did Mary Magdalene return the second time to weep at Jesus' grave? (She did not yet know that Jesus had risen.)
4. To whom did Jesus first appear after he had arisen from the dead? (To Mary Magdalene.)

STORY 59

The Stranger on the Road to Emmaus

Luke 24:13-35; John 20:19-31

The Passover feast had ended, and some of the visitors at Jerusalem were returning to their homes. Along the roadway leading from the city of Jerusalem to the village of Emmaus, seven miles distant, two men were walking slowly, with bowed heads. They were friends of Jesus, and they were troubled about the news that had come to the city just before they started on their journey.

As these men talked together about the trial and crucifixion of Jesus, and about the women's message that early morning, suddenly a stranger joined them and asked, "Why is it that you are so sad? What are you talking about so earnestly?"

The men replied, "Can it be possible that you have not heard about the sad things that have been happening during these few days past?"

And the stranger asked, "What things?"

The men began to tell this stranger about Jesus of Nazareth whom they had hoped would deliver their nation from the rule of the Romans and set up a kingdom. They told him how the chief priests and rulers had

THE STRANGER ON THE ROAD TO EMMAUS

become jealous of him because he was such a mighty prophet, and how they captured him and caused him to be crucified. They told him that Jesus had died on the cross and that his body had been buried by loving friends in a nice, new tomb.

"This is the third day since these things happened," they said, "and this morning some women of our company astonished us by saying they had gone early to the tomb and had seen that his body had been taken away. But they said angels were there, and the angels said he had risen from the dead. Some of our own number hurried to the grave and found that it was indeed empty, but they did not see the angels nor did they see our risen Lord."

The stranger listened patiently, and when they had finished he began to talk to them about the teachings of Moses' law and of the prophets concerning the promised Redeemer of Israel. He showed them by the words of God's book that Jesus, the prophet of Galilee, should suffer these very things and rise again the third day if he would really be the Redeemer for whom they were longing. And the men listened silently, wondering who this stranger could be.

When they came near to the village of Emmaus, the two men asked the stranger to stay with them until the next morning, as the day had nearly ended. So he stopped with them. When they sat down to eat their evening meal he took bread, blessed it, and gave it to them, and they knew at once that he was Jesus, their risen Lord. But he disappeared from their sight.

Now the two men understood why the women who had seen the angels seemed so full of joy. They, too, believed in the risen Lord, and their hearts were filled with gladness. They rose up from the table and hurried back to Jerusalem to tell the disciples that they had seen the Lord.

Questions and Answers

1. About what were the two friends of Jesus talking when they walked toward Emmaus? (The trial and crucifixion of Jesus and the report of his resurrection.)
2. How did these two men recognize Jesus? (When they ate supper, Jesus took bread, blessed it, and gave it to them.)
3. Why did they hasten back to Jerusalem? (They now believed that Jesus was alive and they wanted to tell the others.)

STORY 60

Doubting Thomas

Luke 24:36-48; John 20:19-31

The deep shades of night had fallen over Jerusalem when the two disciples who had seen Jesus at last came to the house where the other disciples and some of their friends were gathered. When they entered the room they saw that a change had come over these people who had been so sad. Now everyone seemed happy, and excited about something. "Jesus is indeed risen," they cried joyously, "for Peter has seen him!" Then the two men told how he had appeared to them on their way to Emmaus, and how they had not known him until he had blessed and broken bread at their evening meal.

While they talked together Jesus himself suddenly appeared in their midst. And they were frightened, for the doors were closed when he entered, and they supposed he was a spirit. But he spoke to them and said, "Why are you fearful? See my hands and my feet; touch me, and see that I am not a spirit, for a spirit does not have flesh and bones as I have."

Then he asked for something to eat, and they gave him a piece of fish and some honey, which he ate before them. Great was their joy on beholding him once more among them, after they had seen him so cruelly tortured and killed.

Thomas, one of the disciples, was not present when Jesus appeared. And he would not believe when the others told him that they had seen the Lord. He said, "Except I see in his hands the print of the nails and put my fingers into the nail prints, and except I thrust my hand into the place where the spear cut his side, I will not believe."

A week passed by, and again the disciples were together in a room, with the doors closed, and this time Thomas was with them. Jesus appeared as suddenly as he had come before and said, "Peace be to you!"

While they were wondering at his strange coming he called Thomas and said, "Behold my hands, and put your finger into the print of the nails; and put your hand into the place where the spear cut my side. And do not doubt, but believe."

Thomas worshiped Jesus, saying, "My Lord, and my God!"

To him Jesus said, "You believe because you have seen; but blessed are those who will believe though they do not see me."

Questions and Answers

1. Which of the Twelve first saw Jesus on the Resurrection day? (Simon Peter.)
2. Who was not present when Jesus appeared to the disciples that evening? (Thomas.)
3. When did Thomas believe Jesus was really alive again? (The first time he saw Jesus.)

STORY 61

Jesus' Last Meeting with His Disciples

Mark 16:15-19; Luke 24:50-53; Acts 1:1-14

Forty days have passed since the Resurrection. During these days Jesus often spoke with his disciples about the kingdom of God. Still they did not understand that it would not be an earthly kingdom, like the kingdom of David. At last the time came for their farewell meeting.

During this time Jesus appeared to his disciples, and "when they saw him, they worshiped him: but some doubted. And Jesus came and spake unto them, saying, All power is given unto me in heaven and in earth. Go ye therefore, and teach all nations, baptizing them in the name of the Father, and of the Son, and of the Holy Ghost."

While they talked earnestly together, Jesus said, "John the Baptist baptized you with water, but you shall be baptized with the Holy Spirit in a few days."

Some of the disciples asked, "Will you at that time restore the kingdom of Israel?"

Jesus said, "It is not for you to know the plans of the heavenly Father; but you shall receive power from heaven when the Holy Spirit comes upon you, and this power will cause you to witness boldly to me in Jerusalem, in all the country of Judea, in Samaria, and in the farthest parts of the world. But do not go away from Jerusalem until the Holy Spirit is given to you."

While Jesus talked to them they were standing together on the Mount of Olives, and suddenly the disciples saw him being caught up into heaven. They watched until he disappeared from sight in bright clouds, after which they saw him no more. But still they stood gazing upward, hoping to catch one more glimpse of their departing Lord. Then two angels came and stood beside them, clothed in beautiful garments of white. They said, "Men of Galilee, why do you stand gazing up into heaven? This same Jesus who is taken up from you into heaven will come again in the same manner as he went away."

Then they left the place and went into Jerusalem, into a room upstairs, where they met together with other friends of Jesus to wait and to pray until the promised Comforter should be given to them. No longer were they sorrowing; great joy filled their hearts because they knew that Jesus is really the Christ.

Questions and Answers

1. Whom did Jesus say he would send to the disciples after he should go away? (Another Comforter.)
2. Where did Jesus have his farewell talk with his disciples? (On the Mount of Olives.)
3. What wonderful event took place there? (Jesus ascended to heaven.)

c.1
Egermeier, Elsie E.
100110 049
Picture-story life of Christ,
GOSHEN COLLEGE-GOOD LIBRARY